This book is the product of

"A study on the English Translation and Introduction of Classical Script of Huangmei Opera"

Chinese-English Version

Lane of Courtesy

Written by Wang Xiaoma

Translated by Wang Qiaoying, Zhu Zhongyan, Wu Jinyi

本书为安徽省教育厅人文社科研究重点项目

“黄梅戏经典剧目英语译介研究”的研究成果

（中英文对照本）

六尺巷

王晓马　著

王巧英　朱忠焰　吴瑾宜　译

全国百佳图书出版单位

时代出版传媒股份有限公司

黄　山　书　社

图书在版编目(CIP)数据

六尺巷:中英文对照本/王晓马著;王巧英,朱忠焰,吴瑾宜译.—合肥:黄山书社,2019.11
ISBN 978-7-5461-8603-0

Ⅰ.①六… Ⅱ.①王… ②王… ③朱… ④吴… Ⅲ.①黄梅戏-剧本-中国-当代-汉、英 Ⅳ.①I236.54

中国版本图书馆 CIP 数据核字(2019)第 271803 号

六尺巷(中英文对照本) 王晓马 著
LIU CHI XIANG(ZHONG YING WEN DUI ZHAO BEN) 王巧英,朱忠焰,吴瑾宜 译

出品人 贾兴权
责任编辑 徐娟娟 熊裕娟
责任印制 李 磊
装帧设计 李 昕
出版发行 时代出版传媒股份有限公司(http://www.press-mart.com)
黄山书社(http://www.hspress.cn)
地址邮编 安徽省合肥市蜀山区翡翠路 1118 号出版传媒广场 7 层 230071
印 刷 安徽联众印刷有限公司
版 次 2019 年 11 月第 1 版
印 次 2019 年 11 月第 1 次印刷
开 本 880mm×1230mm 1/32
字 数 130 千
印 张 5.75
书 号 ISBN 978-7-5461-8603-0
定 价 39.00 元

服务热线 0551-63533706
销售热线 0551-63533761
官方直营书店(http://hsssbook.taobao.com)

目　录

前　言 …… 1

演职表 …… 2

梗　概 …… 6

第一场 …… 8

第二场 …… 42

第三场 …… 76

第四场 …… 102

第五场 …… 126

第六场 …… 148

注　释 …… 168

Contens

Preface 3

Screen Credits 3

Synopsis 7

Act Ⅰ 9

Act Ⅱ 43

Act Ⅲ 77

Act Ⅳ 103

Act Ⅴ 127

Act Ⅵ 149

Notes 168

前 言

六尺巷在“桐城派”的故乡、安徽省桐城市的西南一隅，是一条全长约100米、宽2米的巷道，当地人称之为六尺巷。

史载，三朝宰相张英家旁有隙地一块，与吴氏相邻。吴家欲占用之，张、吴两家遂起纠纷，张家即刻修书进京求助宰相张英。张英看过家书，批诗云：“一纸书来只为墙，让他三尺又何妨？长城万里今犹在，不见当年秦始皇。”

家人得书，遂撤让三尺。吴氏感其义，亦退让三尺，故形成了今天的六尺巷。由此，六尺巷也成为一个文化的载体，其典故所包含的谦和礼让精神实际上也是中华传统文化的精神，黄梅戏经典剧目《六尺巷》正是以此为基础创作而成的。

本书旨在更好地“讲述中国故事”，树立文化自信，向海外传播中华优秀传统文化，弘扬中国传统文化中和谐、谦让的价值观和人生观。因此，对黄梅戏经典剧目《六尺巷》进行汉英对照翻译既能消除语言障碍，加深中国和“一带一路”沿线国家的文化交流与合作；又能帮助沿线国家了解中国传统文化和哲学思想，从而传承和弘扬丝路友好合作精神。

本书是安徽省教育厅人文社科研究重点项目“黄梅戏经典剧目英语译介研究”的研究成果，以“达意”“传神”为总体策略，兼具注重剧本中唱词念白的可阅读性和可演唱性，翻译了黄梅戏经典剧目《六尺巷》。为方便中外读者阅读及理解，译者对剧本中具有中国文化特色的名称、典故、习语等作了英文注释，并根据互联网上广为传播的安庆市黄梅戏剧院一团的完整演出视频，在剧本中唱词念白之前注明了角色名称、旁白以及舞台指示语；为兼顾可演唱性，译者在翻译过程中严格按照中文字数确定英文的音节数，确保译文可以根据曲调演唱。剧本采用中英对照的形式排版，以便读者欣赏。

参与本书翻译的有王巧英、朱忠焰和吴瑾宜。王巧英对译稿进行了反复修改与润色，对全书进行编排；朱忠焰对该剧本的英译给予了指导，审阅了全书译文，为该书的出版提供了帮助。本书在翻译过程中得到了安庆师范大学外国语学院党委书记郝涂根的大力支持；著名黄梅戏编剧王晓马提供了黄梅戏《六尺巷》剧本并授权同意翻译；黄山书社有关同志对本书的编辑与出版付出了辛勤的劳动；借此机会对他们一并表示感谢。

鉴于译者的知识水平和所掌握的黄梅戏翻译资料有限，书中难免存在错误和不妥之处，恳请专家和读者批评指正。

译　者

2019 年 7 月 15 日

Preface

In the southwest corner of Tongcheng City, Anhui Province, the hometown of Tongcheng School, lies a lane of about 100 meters long and two meters wide. The local people call it the Lane of Courtesy.

According to historic records, there was a vacant lot beside the house of Zhang Ying, the Prime Minister for Three Emperors, adjacent to Wu's house. Because the Wus wanted to occupy it, the two families had a dispute. Immediately, the Zhangs sent a letter to the capital to ask Minister Zhang Ying for help. After reading the letter from home, Zhang Ying wrote a poem which read: "Write to me just for a wall. Why not offer him three Chi of land? Now the Great Wall still stands there, but the First Emperor doesn't exist."

Zhang's family received the letter and moved the wall back for three Chi. Moved by his righteousness, the Wus also did so. Consequently, the present Lane of Courtesy came into being. As a result, the Lane of Courtesy has also become a carrier of culture. The spirit of modesty and courtesy contained in this allusion is actually the spirit of Chinese traditional culture. The classic repertoire "Lane of Courtesy", a Huangmei Opera, is based on this allusion.

This book aims at "telling the Chinese story" better, establishing cultural self-confidence, spreading excellent Chinese traditional culture and promoting the values and outlook on harmony and humility in Chinese traditional culture. Therefore, on the one hand, the Chinese-English translation of the classic Huangmei Opera "Lane of Courtesy" can eliminate language barrier, deepen the cultural exchanges and cooperation between China and the countries along the Belt and Road. On the other hand, it can help the countries along the line to understand Chinese traditional culture and philosophical thoughts so as to inherit and carry forward the spirit of friendship and cooperation along the Silk Road.

As the product of "A study on the English Translation and Introduction of Classical Script of Huangmei Opera", a key project of the Humanities and Social Sciences Research of the Education Bureau of Anhui Province, "Lane of Courtesy", a classic script of Huangmei Opera, is translated according to the general strategy of achieving both faithfulness and expressiveness, with the focus on the readability and singability of the lyrics in the translation. In order to facilitate the reading and understanding for Chinese and foreign readers, the translators make English notes on the names, allusions and idioms with typical Chinese cultural features in the script, and mark out each role for the lyrics, narration and stage directions in the script according to the complete performance video of No. One Troupe of Anqing Municipal Theater of Huangmei Opera, which is widely spread on the Internet. In order to balance the singability, the translators determine the number of syllables of English words in strict accordance to the number of Chinese characters in the translation process, to ensure that the English translation can be sung in the tune of Huangmei Opera. The book is formatted in Chinese and English, with illustrations and stage photos related to the theme or session for appreciation.

The translators of the book are Wang Qiaoying, Zhu Zhongyan and Wu Jinyi. Wang Qiaoying is responsible for repeated revision and retouching of the translation, and typesetting the whole book; Zhu Zhongyan gives guidance on the English translation of the script, reviews the translation of the book, and provides help for the publication of the book. Wang Xiaoma, the famous playwright of Huangmei Opera, provided the script of "Lane of Courtesy" and granted us the translation permission. Besides, this book receives constant support from Hao Tugen, the Party Secretary of the School of Foreign Languages, Anqing Normal University, and continuous efforts by Huangshan Press. Deepest gratitude is felt towards all of them.

Owing to the limited capacity of translators and inadequate existing translation materials of Huangmei Opera, perhaps errors still exist in this book here and there. We sincerely welcome criticisms, corrections and observations from experts and readers.

Translators

July 15, 2019

六 尺 巷

Lane of Courtesy

演职表

编　剧:王晓马

导　演:李　杰

作　曲:陈华庆

配　器:韦　宁

指　挥:汪玉龙

打击乐设计:夏积成

舞蹈设计:张文林

舞美设计:蔡欣平

灯光设计:蔡传厚　江向东

服装设计:张豫美

人物造型设计:王　红

道具设计:万玉生　徐　俊

效果设计:马甲甲　肖　汉

Screen Credits

Playwright: Wang Xiaoma

Director: Li Jie

Music: Chen Huaqing

Instrumentation: Wei Ning

Conductor: Wang Yulong

Percussion design: Xia Jicheng

Choreography: Zhang Wenlin

Stage Design: Cai Xinping

Lighting Design: Cai Chuanhou, Jiang Xiangdong

Costume Design: Zhang Yumei

Design of Character Figures: Wang Hong

Property Design: Wan Yusheng, Xu Jun

Effect Design: Ma Jiajia, Xiao Han

徐　娘 — 张小萍

徐昌茂 — 潘文庆

张天昊 — 崔克勇

吴和成 — 董家林

徐夫人 — 白　红

茗　奴 — 张　丽

衙役甲 — 马　丁

衙役乙 — 黄少勇

乡绅甲 — 阚根华

乡绅乙 — 汪金才

乡绅丙 — 龚洪涛

司　鼓 — 夏积成

主　音 — 周永忠

安庆市黄梅戏剧院一团演出

Xu Niang—Zhang Xiaoping

Xu Changmao—Pan Wenqing

Zhang Tianhao—Cui Keyong

Wu Hecheng—Dong Jialin

Mrs. Xu—Bai Hong

Ming Nu—Zhang Li

Yamen Runner A—Ma Ding

Yamen Runner B—Huang Shaoyong

Squire A—Kan Genhua

Squire B—Wang jingcai

Squire C—Gong Hongtao

Drum—Xia Jicheng

Keynote—Zhou Yongzhong

Performed by No. One Troupe of

Anqing Municipal Theater of Huangmei Opera

梗 概

六尺巷在“桐城派[1]”的故乡、安徽省桐城市的西南一隅，是一条全长约100米、宽2米的巷道，当地人称之为六尺巷。

史载，三朝宰相[2] 张英家旁有隙地一块，与吴氏相邻。吴家欲占用之，张、吴两家遂起纠纷，张家即刻修书进京求助宰相张英。张英看过家书，批诗云：一纸书来只为墙，让他三尺[3] 又何妨？长城万里今犹在，不见当年秦始皇。

家人得书，遂撤让三尺。吴氏感其义，亦退让三尺，故形成了今天的六尺巷。

旁　白　人之初，性本善。
　　　　性相近，习相远。
　　　　苟不教，性乃迁。
　　　　教之道，贵以专。
　　　　昔孟母，择邻处。[4]

Synopsis

In the southwest corner of Tongcheng City, Anhui Province, the hometown of Tongcheng School[1], lies a lane of about 100 meters long and two meters wide. The local people call it the Lane of Courtesy.

According to historic records, there was a vacant lot beside the house of Zhang Ying, the Prime Minister for Three Emperors[2], adjacent to Wu's house. Because the Wus wanted to occupy it, the Zhangs and the Wus had a dispute. Immediately, the Zhangs sent a letter to the capital to ask Minister Zhang Ying for help. After reading the letter from home, Zhang Ying replied a poem which read: Write to me just for a wall. Why not offer him three Chi[3] land? Now the Great Wall still stands there, But the First Emperor doesn't exist.

His family received the letter and moved the wall back for three Chi. Moved by his righteousness, the Wus also did so. Consequently, the present Lane of Courtesy came into being.

Voice-over Man on earth, good at birth.
The same nature, varies on nurture.
With no education, there'd be aberration.
To teach well, you deeply dwell.
Then Mencius' mother, chose her neighbor.[4]

第一场

张天昊　（白）哈哈！

　　　　这傩戏[5]唱得好！

　　　　跳得好！

　　　　打赏！

　　　　打赏！

旁　白　汪秀才[6]到！

汪秀才　（白）老管家！

张天昊　（白）汪秀才！

旁　白　徐秀才到！

张天昊　（白）哎呀，徐秀才！

旁　白　唐老先生到！

张天昊　（白）哎呀，唐老先生！

　　　　乡绅甲（点头）

　　　　乡绅乙、丙（上）

张天昊　（白）哎呀，来了！

众乡绅　（白）恭喜老管家！贺喜老管家！

张天昊　（白）同喜同喜呀！

乡绅甲　（白）恭喜恭喜！

Act I

Zhang Tianhao	(speak) Haha!
	Well sung! The Nuo Opera[5]!
	Well danced!
	Reward!
	Reward!
Voice-over	Here comes Xiucai[6] Wang!
Xiucai Wang	(speak) Hi! Old butler!
Zhang Tianhao	(speak) Hi! Xiucai Wang!
Voice-over	Here comes Xiucai Xu!
Zhang Tianhao	(speak) Hi! Xiucai Xu!
Voice-over	Here comes Mr. Tang the Sr.!
Zhang Tianhao	(speak) Hi! Mr. Tang the Sr.!
	Squire A (nodding)
	Squire B and C (onstage)
Zhang Tianhao	(speak) Hi! You're here!
Squires	(speak) Congratulations!
	Congratulations!
Zhang Tianhao	(speak) Thank you for your congratulation!
Squire A	(speak) Congratulations!

老管家，

相爷拜文华殿大学士[7]啊，

又要重修相府大屋，

真乃可喜可贺哇！

众乡绅　（白）可喜可贺哇！

张天昊　（白）同喜同喜！

全托皇上洪福，

皇恩浩荡哪！

哈哈哈哈！

老先生，

老朽为贺相爷荣升，

重修相府老宅，

西墙可要占府上

东院一砖之地哟。

乡绅乙　（白）哎，别说一砖之地，

就是十砖百砖又有何妨啊？

哪个叫他与相爷是

少时同窗哪。

乡绅丙　（白）就是就是嘛！

乡绅乙　（白）相爷荣升

Old butler,

The Minister is pointed as grand secretary of Wenhua Hall[7]

And the Minister's mansion is to be rebuilt.

Many congratulations to you!

Squires	(speak) Congratulations!
Zhang Tianhao	(speak) Thank you for your congratulations!
	Thanks to the Emperor,
	Mighty royal grace!
	Haha haha!
	Senior mister,
	To celebrate his promotion,
	The old house is to be rebuilt.
	The west wall might occupy a space
	Of one brick of your east yard.
Squire B	(speak) Hey, just a space of one brick,
	How about a space of even ten or one hundred bricks?
	Everybody knows he is the schoolmate
	Of the Minister.
Squire C	(speak) I can not agree more!
Squire B	(speak) His promotion

乃我县之荣耀也。
老管家重修相府老屋，
我等要人尽其力，
这地尽其材呀。
老先生，
你说是也不是呀？

乡绅甲　（白）那是，那是！（故意以拐棍顿地，打到乡绅乙的脚）

乡绅乙　（跛至一旁，以手抚脚）哎哟，哎哟！

张天昊　（白）又要扰动乡邻了。

乡绅丙　（白）老管家，老管家，
相爷能有今天，
邻里也光彩嘛！
哪有什么
打扰乡里一说呢？

张天昊　（白）哎呀，老朽[8]先替相爷
谢谢诸位乡邻了。
诸位日后有什么想法，
有什么大事要办，
只管开口，
只要老朽给相爷

Is the glory of our county.
Now the old house is to be rebuilt,
Each of us should try our best
To do what we can do.
Senior mister,
Do you agree with me or not?

Squire A (speak) Sure, sure! (Squire A knocks the floor with his stick, purposefully hits the foot of squire B)

Squire B (walk lamely aside and touch his foot with his hand) Ouch, ouch!

Zhang Tianhao (speak) You neighbors will be disturbed again.

Squire C (speak) Old butler, old butler,
Now the Minister's glory
Is shining the neighbors too!
How can you say
You're disturbing the neighborhood?

Zhang Tianhao (speak) Alas, the dotage[8] thanks neighbors
In the name of the Minister.
If you have any ideas or want to do
Any big deals in the future,
Just tell me,
So long as the dotage writes

一封书信……

乡绅乙　(白)哎呀,

那就多谢大管家关照哇!

张天昊　(白)里面请,里面请!

众乡绅　(白)好好好,请请请!(乡绅甲一旁退下)

张天昊　(追赶,白)哎,哎,老先生,老先生!

乡绅甲　(白)告退,告退!

张天昊　(唱)天生社稷真卿相,

众仆役　(唱)真呀么真卿相,

张天昊　(唱)才称朝廷做栋梁。

众仆役　(唱)做呀么做栋梁。

张天昊　(唱)万岁[9]又把金爵赏,

众仆役　(唱)金爵赏哪,

张天昊　(唱)桐城县从此天下

美呀美名扬啊,

众仆役　(唱)美名扬啊,美名扬啊,

张天昊　(唱)美名扬!哈哈哈哈!

旁　白　知县[10]大人、夫人到!

徐夫人　(上)老管家,

恭喜恭喜呀!

To the Minister…

Squire B (speak) Alas,

Thanks a lot for the butler's special note!

Zhang Tianhao (speak) Come in please! Come in please!

Squires (speak) All right. Please, please! (Squire A walks offstage.)

Zhang Tianhao (chase after and speak) Hey, hey, senior mister, senior mister!

Squire A (speak) Excuse myself, excuse myself!

Zhang Tianhao (sing) He's a natural Minister,

Menservants (sing) A natural Minister,

Zhang Tianhao (sing) The court's talented pillar.

Menservants (sing) The talented pillar.

Zhang Tianhao (sing) His Majesty[9] rewards him again,

Menservants (sing) Rewards him again,

Zhang Tianhao (sing) From now on our Tongcheng County

Becomes famous for ever,

Menservants (sing) Famous for ever, famous for ever.

Zhang Tianhao (sing) Famous now! Haha! Haha!

Voice-over Here come Magistrate[10] and Lady!

Mrs. Xu (onstage) Old butler,

Congratulations!

徐昌茂　（上）老管家，

大喜大喜呀！

张天昊　（白）老爷，夫人，同喜同喜呀！

徐昌茂　（白）老管家，

相府老宅重修之事

就按你讲的办吧！（徐昌茂递过礼单，张天昊心有疑虑，接过礼单打开朗读）

张天昊　（白）西墙西移一尺，

东墙东扩一丈[11]，

北墙北移。

哎呀，抬举，

大人[12]真是抬举老朽了！

徐昌茂　（白）此乃是本县份内之劳，

也算是下官

为贺相爷荣升

敬献的一份薄礼吧。

张天昊　（白）如此，

我就择定黄道吉日[13]

开工啰？

徐昌茂　（白）开工！

张天昊　（白）开工？

Xu Changmao	(onstage) Old butler, Great rejoicings!
Zhang Tianhao	(speak) Master, Lady, thank you for your congratulations!
Xu Changmao	(speak) Old butler, The renovation of the old mansion Will be done as you said! (Xu Changmao passes a list of present to Zhang Tianhao who receives it and reads doubtfully)
Zhang Tianhao	(speak) Move the west wall one chi westward, Move the east wall one zhang[11] eastward, Move the north wall northward. Alas, favor, My Lord[12] really favors the dotage!
Xu Changmao	(speak) This is what the magistrate should do, Also this can be a Meagre present from me For the Minister's promotion.
Zhang Tianhao	(speak) In that case, I will choose an auspicious day[13] To start?
Xu Changmao	(speak) Start!
Zhang Tianhao	(speak) Start?

徐昌茂	(白)开工!
张天昊、徐昌茂	(大笑)哈哈哈!
徐夫人	(白)老管家, 都说你人老手嫩, 办事总是少把劲。 这一回重修这相府老宅, 相爷把你看的斗大牛粗。 你可要精心点, 细心点,扎干点, 莫把事情做砸了。
徐昌茂	(白)哎,你这个乌鸦嘴![14]
张天昊	(白)夫人总爱说笑, 不碍事,不碍事。
徐夫人	(白)老管家……(知县在后以折扇敲之,知县夫人回头停顿)喂哎!
徐夫人	(唱)都说你人老无用, 手笨脚也笨哪。
张天昊	(唱)讲得我一口恶气 憋,憋,憋半生!
徐昌茂	(唱)这一回重修宰相府……
张天昊	(唱)相爷把千斤重担

Xu Changmao	(speak) Start!
Zhang Tianhao and Xu Changmao	(laugh) Hahaha!
Mrs. Xu	(speak) Old butler, They say you're old and tender, Always less energetic. This time to rebuild the Minister's house, The Minister sees you as a big man. You'd better be careful, Chary and competent to Make sure not to screw things up.
Xu Changmao	(speak) Hey, what a corvine mouth[14] you're!
Zhang Tianhao	(speak) Lady is always joking, Never mind, never mind.
Mrs. Xu	(speak) Old butler … (The magistrate is behind her, knocking her with his folded fan. Lady Xu turns her head back and pauses) Hey, why!
Mrs. Xu	(sing) It's said you're old and useless, With clumsy hands and feet.
Zhang Tianhao	(sing) What she said makes me angry But, I, can not say!
Xu Changmao	(sing) This time to rebuild the mansion …
Zhang Tianhao	(sing) The Minister hands me alone

交我一个人。

徐昌茂 （唱）我说生姜还是老的辣。[15]

徐昌茂、徐夫人 （白）这一回呀，

你要出他个满堂彩。[16]

徐昌茂、徐夫人、张天昊 （唱）亮一亮你（我）的大才能！

张天昊 （白）此次相府重修，北墙北移，

与老爷小妹府上的南墙……

徐昌茂 （白）不碍事，不碍事哟！

小妹家的南墙，

它就是天生地长，

也不能影响

相府老宅扩建哪！

徐夫人 （白）扩建！

不是说好重修吗？

怎么一下子工夫，

变成了扩建？

徐昌茂 （白）呃，重修就是扩建，

扩建就是重修。

一回事，一回事嘛。

徐夫人 （白）一回事？

	The heavy burden.
Xu Changmao	(sing) Veterans are wiser than recruits.[15]
Xu Changmao and Mrs. Xu	(speak) This is the time For you to perform excellently.[16]
Xu Changmao, Mrs.Xu and Zhang Tianhao	(sing) Make a full play of your (my) talents!
Zhang Tianhao	(speak) Since the rebuilding will move the north wall, The south wall of the house of your sister…
Xu Changmao	(speak) No, no, no, not in the way! Even though the south wall of My sister naturally exists, It shouldn't hinder The old mansion's extension!
Mrs. Xu	(speak) Extension! Isn't it to be rebuilt? How can it be suddenly Turned into extension?
Xu Changmao	(speak) Haw, rebuilding is extension, Extension is rebuilding. They're the same, they are the same.
Mrs. Xu	(speak) They're the same?

那你的意思是说，
猫就是狗，狗就是猫？
哦！我晓得着，
怪不得前几天
你要我去小妹家，
把扩建南墙的
官批牒文要回来，
原来是为了……

徐昌茂　(白)哎哟，行了！
小妹家南墙
它不是好好的吗？
建什么建？
修什么修？
都跟你一样，
没有事找事！

徐夫人　(白)你才没事找事！
这事要是让
小妹和姑爷[17]知道了，
我看你……

吴和成　(吟唱)人之初，性本善。

So what you are saying is
That cats are dogs and dogs are cats?
Oh! I know it now.
No wonder on that day
You asked me to get back
The official warrant
For extension from sister.
It turned out to be for…

Xu Changmao (speak) Oh, dear! Okay!
Isn't the south wall of
My sister's house in good condition?
What to be built?
What to be repaired?
Just the same as you,
She is asking for trouble!

Mrs. Xu (speak) It's you who is asking for trouble!
If it is known by
Your sister and brother-in-law, [17]
I think you…

Wu Hecheng (chant) Man on earth, good at birth.

吴和成　（吟诵）人之初，性本善。

性相近，习相远。

苟不教……

徐昌茂　（白）呃，姑爷。

吴和成　（吟诵）哼！性乃迁。

教之道，贵以专。

昔孟母，择邻处。

昔孟母，择邻处。

徐昌茂　（白）哎，姑爷。

吴和成　（吟诵）择邻处！择邻处，择邻处……（边诵边下）

徐昌茂　（白）这江山易主都几十年了，

他竟不知改弦更张，

还是这样不识时务。

哼！

老管家，

我们家姑爷

他不是个明白人。

莫跟他计较。

张天昊　（白）不与计较，不与计较。

知县大人为相府重修，

Wu Hecheng	(intone) Man on earth, good at birth.
	The same nature, varies on nurture.
	With no education …
Xu Changmao	(speak) Hem, brother-in-law.
Wu Hecheng	(intone) Hum! There'd be aberration.
	To teach well, you deeply dwell.
	Then Mencius' mother, chose her neighbor.
	Then Mencius' mother, chose her neighbor.
Xu Changmao	(speak) Hey, brother-in-law.
Wu Hecheng	(intone) Chose her neighbor! Chose her neighbor!
	Chose her neighbor… (goes offstage)
Xu Changmao	(speak) The ownership has been changed for decades,
	He didn't know how to mend his way,
	Still remaining behind the times.
	Hum!
	Old butler,
	Our brother-in-law
	Is not a sensible man.
	Don't fuss about him.
Zhang Tianhao	(speak) Not be fussed about, not be fussed about.
	For the rebuilding, you Magistrate

把准许自己妹妹家

重葺南墙的牒文收回。

此情此意，

老朽是心知肚明。

只是……

徐昌茂　（白）老管家尽放宽心。

我们家姑爷不是明白人，

我家小妹可是通情达理，

对什么事都明明白白。

在那个家里面，

可是我家小妹说了算。

再说，

我和我家小妹间的关系，

你是知道的。

只要我一句话……

张天昊　（白）老朽修书，

老朽立马修书禀告相爷。

大人、夫人，

里面请，请。

诸位，

Withdrew the official warrant
For repairing your sister's south wall.
The dotage knows
Your tender regards clearly.
However…

Xu Changmao (speak) Old butler, just be relaxed.
Although my brother-in-law is not sensible
My little sister is reasonable so
She knows everything clearly and plainly.
It's my little sister
Who has the last word in that family.
What's more,
You do know the relationship between
My sister and me.
Just one word from me is…

Zhang Tianhao (speak) I will write to
The Minister to report it at once.
My lord and lady,
Come in please, please.
Everybody,

知县大人和夫人驾到！

鼓乐相迎！

茗　奴　（急跑上）歇着！歇着！

三天了，

吵得偌大一个桐城

猫狗都不能安生！

徐昌茂　（白）茗奴！

茗　奴　（白）舅爷，

我们家老爷的病

就是他们家给吵犯的。

徐夫人　（白）啊？他和成又犯毛病了？

茗　奴　（白）怪的就是他。

我家老爷这几年

都没有犯过病了，

书馆也开的好好的。

这几天，他们家

又是锣又是鼓，

又是炮仗又是铳！

吵得耗子进洞，

猫不吃荤，

Here come the Magistrate and the Lady!
Welcome with music!

Mingnu (Hurriedly onstage) Stop it! Stop it!
Such a large
Tongcheng has been noisy for three days.
Even cats and dogs have no peace!

Xu Changmao (speak) Mingnu!

Mingnu (speak) Master-uncle,
My master has an attack
Of his old illness caused by their noise.

Mrs. Xu (speak) What? Hecheng is having one of his turns?

Mingnu (speak) He's the one to blame.
In recent years, my master
Has not fallen ill at all,
And has run his private school well.
In these days, they have made
Such noise with gongs and drums,
Firecrackers and blunderbusses!
It's so noisy that mice stay
In holes and cats

一个桐城县吵得

都不得安宁！

一人得道，鸡犬升天。

哼！（茗奴下）

张天昊　（白）你，你你……

徐夫人　（白）哎哟，不好着，这变天着喂，

要下雨啦。

哎哟，老管家，

你真背。

你的运气呀，

也是不太好喂！

旁白　南墙倒喽！

吴府的南墙倒喽！

茗　奴　（白）夫人，

南墙又倒着。

徐　娘　（白）倒了，倒得好！

吴和成　（白）好！呜呼哉！呵呵呵！好！

吴和成　（唱）好得很喏——

仆役甲　（白）怪！

我家相爷升回官，

Don't eat fish, with the whole county

Having no peace at all!

One's promotion uplifts his men.

Hum! (Mingnu goes offstage)

Zhang Tianhao (speak) You, you, you…

Mrs. Xu (speak) Oops! It's not fine. The weather is changing.

It's going to rain.

Oops! Old butler,

You're unlucky.

Indeed, your luck is

Not so good, either!

Voice-over Down the south wall!

Down the south wall of the Wu's!

Mingnu (speak) Lady,

The south wall is down again.

Xu Niang (speak) Down again? It's quite good!

Wu Hecheng (speak) Good! Alack! Heh Heh Heh! Good!

Wu Hecheng (sing) It is quite good!

Manservant A (speak) Strange!

Our minister's promotion

他吴府就倒回墙。

仆役乙　(白)你讲得还真在理！

我家相爷

选翰林[18]的时候啊，

他家墙也倒了。

仆役丙　(白)哎哎，我还听说啊，

我们家老爷

中状元[19]那一年哪，

他们家的南墙也倒了。

这一回相爷官拜大学士[20]，

这不，墙又倒着。

仆役甲　(白)这墙总倒有六七回了。

仆役乙　(白)不对，何止六七回，

起码也有八九回了。

仆役甲　(白)哎，六七回。

仆役乙　(白)八九回。

仆役甲　(白)六七回，

仆役乙　(白)八九回！(茗奴驱赶)

仆役甲　(白)哎！哈哈哈！(众仆役下)

吴和成　(白)天意，天意哟。

Follows with the Wu's wall down.

Manservant B (speak) What you said is sensible!

When our Minister

Was selected as Hanlin,[18]

His wall also fell down.

Manservant C (speak) Hey hey, I also heard when

That year our master

Was selected as Zhuangyuan[19],

The south wall of their house fell down too.

Now the Minister is conferred Daxueshi[20],

You see the wall down again.

Manservant A (speak) The wall might fall down six or seven times.

Manservant B (speak) No, more than six or seven times,

At least it had eight or nine times.

Manservant A (speak) Oh, six or seven.

Manservant B (speak) Eight or nine.

Manservant A (speak) Six or seven.

Manservant B (speak) Eight or nine. (Mingnu drives them away)

Manservant A (speak) Oh! Hahaha! (Menservants go offstage)

Wu Hecheng (speak) God's will, it's god's will

每每他家有喜，
我家有祸。
他家有喜，我家有祸。
他家有喜，我家有祸。
他家有喜，我家有祸……

徐　娘　（白）和成！

茗　奴　（白）姑爷！

徐　娘　（白）你看你！想到哪里去了。

徐　娘　（唱）倒了南墙不可怕，
心里的南墙不能塌。
灰砖白泥再和上，
新颜替旧貌，
南墙更焕发。
南墙里有一块
我们的天地，
天地里
有我们的夫妻情长。
这一回重葺南墙，
我再筹划。
这一回就是

Every time joy in his house,
Woe in my house.
Joy in his house, woe in my house.
Joy in his house, woe in my house.
Joy in his house, woe in my house…

Xu Niang (speak) Hecheng!

Mingnu (speak) Master!

Xu Niang (speak) Look at you! You must have a wrong thought.

Xu Niang (sing) The fallen wall isn't terrible,
But the wall in mind can't collapse.
Again rebuild the south wall with
Gray bricks and white mud,
It'll be more shining.
In the south wall there is
A piece of our world,
Which contains
Our affection as man and wife.
For the south wall's rebuilding,
I'll make a plan.
This time I'll make it

要比那相府强，
比那相府强。

吴和成　（白）命里只有九角九，
走遍天下不满升。

吴和成　（唱）焕发不焕发，
什么强不强。
运去黄金变锈铁，
抬腿就遇鬼（那个鬼）打墙。
你把这俗话细掂量，
万事自会有主张。
天机太玄妙，
谁也说不出一二三，
万事随缘。

徐　娘　（白）和成。

吴和成　（白）唉，
想我吴府
自改朝换代以来，
谨遵祖宗遗训，
绝了仕途，开馆讲学。
自从张家入朝，

Better than Minister's,
Better than they do.

Wu Hecheng (speak) It is your predestined fate,
Wherever you go, it won't change.

Wu Hecheng (sing) To shine or not shine,
Be better or not.
When one's luck departs from him,
His gold would turn into rusty iron.
If you think over the old saying,
You'll have an idea of everything.
The nature's mystery
Is too hard for anyone to tell.
Everything goes well.

Xu Niang (speak) Hecheng.

Wu Hecheng (speak) Well,
I think that I,
Since the reform of dynasties,
Have obeyed my ancestors
And ceased career to give lectures.
Since the Zhangs entered the court,

我吴府总也不顺。

与他真乃是地煞对天罡，[21]

犯的就是相。[22]

徐　娘　(白)和成，

有道是井水不犯河水。

他走他的阳关道，

我过我的独木桥。

你满腹经纶教书育人，

也是大道正业。

千万不可自缠苦结，

灰心丧志啊。

明日我就到县府衙门，

去找我那兄长。

吴和成　(白)他？哼哼哼！

当年与我歃血盟誓，

不仕清廷的是他；

现今顶戴花翎[23]，

风光无限的也是他。

前日官批牒文，

许你南墙的是他；

I have nothing smooth at all.
He and I are like Disha to Tiangang[21],
Which go against each other.[22]

Xu Niang (speak) Hecheng,
It's said each one minds his business.
He takes the broad road and I
Will cross the single-log bridge.
Your teaching with your profound learning
Is also legitimate.
Never have yourself entangled hard,
And don't lose your heart.
Tomorrow I'll go to my brother
In the Yamen for help.

Wu Hecheng (speak) He? Hum Hum Hum!
It was he who once took blood oath
With me not to serve the court;
Now it's also him who wears
Peacock plume[23] and enjoy great honour.
It was he who gave you
The south wall warrant that day;

昨日收墙收地，
另许他家的还是他！
算了，算了！
天不佑我，地不佑我，
墙——不佑我。
闭馆休学，
我，走！

徐　娘　（白）啊，和成！
和成，你要到哪里去？

吴和成　（白）路漫漫兮而修远，
吾将上下而求索。
走！哈哈哈哈！

徐　娘　（白）和成，和成，
和成，和成……

It was also he who took
It all back for others yesterday!
Drop it, drop it!
Neither God nor the earth blesses me!
So — does the wall.
Just close the school,
I'll go!

Xu Niang (speak) Oh, Hecheng!
Hecheng, where are you leaving for?

Wu Hecheng (speak) Though it's a long way to go,
I'll seek the truth up and down.
Go! Hahahaha!

Xu Niang (speak) Hecheng, Hecheng,
Hecheng, Hecheng…

第二场

徐夫人　（白）哎哟，你快一点、快一点着！

徐昌茂　（白）来着嘛。

徐夫人　（白）快一点着！

哎哟，快点快点，

你快点！

徐昌茂　（白）你催，你催！

我的个妈妈吔，

你催么事！

徐夫人　（白）不是你讲，

要到小妹家看看去吗？

徐昌茂　（白）是呀！

不过……

好好好，走走走。

徐夫人　（白）哎哎哎，你你你……

噢，心虚！

你心虚了吧！

徐昌茂　（白）我心虚么东西呀？

徐夫人　（白）你自己清楚！

不做亏心事，

Act II

Mrs. Xu	(speak) Oh, dear! Can't you hurry up? Hurry up! Come on!
Xu Changmao	(speak) I'm coming!
Mrs. Xu	(speak) Hurry up! Come on! Oh, my! Hurry up!, Hurry up! Just hurry up!
Xu Changmao	(speak) You just urge, urge! For goodness' sake! Why do You keep urging me?!
Mrs. Xu	(speak) Didn't you say you Were going to the little sister's house?
Xu Changmao	(speak) Oh, yes! However … Well, well, well, go, go, go.
Mrs. Xu	(speak) Hey, hey, hey, you… Oh, you're guilty! You must be guilty now!
Xu Changmao	(speak) What is it I feel guilty about?
Mrs. Xu	(speak) You know it yourself! A quiet conscience can

不怕鬼敲门。
怪不得你慢慢腾腾，
磨磨蹭蹭拖拖拉拉，
晃晃悠悠唧唧磨磨。

徐昌茂　（白）行了，去看小妹，
我是巴不得立马就到。
可是一想起那位
抱着葫芦不开瓢——
死脑筋的姑爷……

徐夫人　（白）姑爷他呀，
他是守着先人遗训，
是好孝心。

徐昌茂　（白）死脑筋。

徐夫人　（白）好孝心。

徐昌茂　（白）死脑筋！

徐夫人　（白）好孝心！

徐昌茂　（白）死脑筋！

衙役甲　（白）老爷、夫人，
姑娘来着。

徐昌茂　（白）小妹来着？

	Sleep well in thunder.
	No wonder you stroll and slug,
	Lounge and loaf, delay and drag,
	Stagger and sway, hesitate and halt.
Xu Changmao	(speak) All right, to see sister,
	I only wish I could be there right away.
	But when I think of her man
	Who is as much stubborn as
	A block-headed donkey…
Mrs. Xu	(speak) Brother-in-law
	Follows his ancestors' teachings.
	He's very filial.
Xu Changmao	(speak) Block-headed.
Mrs. Xu	(speak) Very filial.
Xu Changmao	(speak) Block-headed!
Mrs. Xu	(speak) Very filial!
Xu Changmao	(speak) Block-headed!
Yamen Runner A	(speak) Master, lady,
	Your sister comes.
Xu Changmao	(speak) Does my sister come?

徐夫人	（白）小妹来着？
衙役甲	（白）来着。
徐夫人	（白）快请，快请！
衙役甲	（白）有请姑娘——
徐　娘	（白）嫂嫂，兄长。
徐夫人、徐昌茂	（白）小妹来着， 来，快坐，坐坐坐。
徐昌茂	（白）哎呀，小妹呀， 我和你嫂嫂 正准备到府上去看望。
徐夫人	（白）小妹呀， 和成的病怎么样了？
徐　娘	（白）又犯了。
徐昌茂	（白）那南墙？
徐　娘	（白）又倒了。
徐昌茂	（白）还真的倒了？
徐夫人	（白）倒了正好， 正好扩建。
徐昌茂	（白）不是扩建是重修。
徐夫人	（白）重修就是扩建，

Mrs. Xu	(speak) Does my sister come?
Yamen Runner A	(speak) Yes, she does.
Mrs. Xu	(speak) Come in, please!
Yamen Runner A	(speak) Come in, please!
Xu Niang	(speak) Sister-in-law, brother.
Mrs. Xu and Xu Changmao	(speak) Sister is here.
	Come on, sit down, sit down.
Xu Changmao	(speak) Well, little sister,
	Your sister-in-law
	And I are going to your house to visit.
Mrs. Xu	(speak) Dear sister,
	How's Hecheng's illness at present?
Xu Niang	(speak) He's ill again.
Xu Changmao	(speak) The south wall?
Xu Niang	(speak) It fell again.
Xu Changmao	(speak) It really fell again?
Mrs. Xu	(speak) Fell just in time
	For extension.
Xu Changmao	(speak) No, not extend but rebuild.
Mrs. Xu	(speak) Rebuilding is extending.

扩建就是重修！
猫就是狗，
狗就是猫！

徐昌茂　（白）哎哟，你还有完没有完哪。

徐夫人　（白）完了完了。
小妹呀，小妹，
你哥哥晓得你是无事不登三宝殿，
有什么话呀，你就讲。

徐　娘　（白）兄长，嫂子。

徐　娘　（唱）你知我从不开那求人口，
你知我从不低那求人头。
我本想将将就就来度日月，
我本想藏起天下的忧和愁。
岂知老天不长眼，
总把灾祸信手丢。
风雨又把南墙倒，
不得不来把我的哥哥求。

徐夫人　（白）小妹呀，小妹呀，
你是姑娘他是老舅，
这姑娘老舅本是一家。

Extending is rebuilding!

A cat is a dog.

A dog is a cat!

Xu Changmao (speak) Oh, my! You have not finished your words yet?

Mrs. Xu (speak) Finished, finished.

Dear little sister,

Your brother knows you will not come here without any requirement.

Just tell him what you want to say.

Xu Niang (speak) Brother, sister-in-law.

Xu Niang (sing) You know that I haven't pleaded with others for help,

And you know I haven't bowed my head for aid.

I had wanted to put up with the living,

And I had wanted to hide all the sorrow.

But who knows the careless God

Throw disasters here and there.

The storm blew down the south wall,

So I have to come to my brother for help.

Mrs. Xu (speak) My dear little sister,

You and he are the aunt and uncle,

And you were born in the same family.

你呀，要什么东西就说，
有什么话就讲。
讲出来呀，
你哥哥他一定帮！

徐　娘　（白）兄长。

徐昌茂　（白）哎？对，一定帮。

徐　娘　（白）真的？

徐昌茂　（白）真的。

徐　娘　（白）讲话算话？

徐昌茂　（白）肯定算话。

徐　娘　（白）扯谎是小狗！

徐昌茂　（白）哦，你还有心思讲笑。
有话就讲，
什么猫呀狗的。

徐　娘　（白）不，我要你讲
哪个扯谎，
哪个就是小狗。

徐昌茂　（白）好好好，
哪个扯谎，
哪个就是小狗。

So, just tell him anything you want and
Any words you want to say.
If you speak out,
Your brother must help you out!

Xu Niang (speak) Dear brother.

Xu Changmao (speak) Well? Sure, I'll help you.

Xu Niang (speak) Really?

Xu Changmao (speak) Really.

Xu Niang (speak) You bet that's so?

Xu Changmao (speak) I bet that's so.

Xu Niang (speak) A liar is shameless!

Xu Changmao (speak) Well, you're still in the mood to laugh.
Speak out your words,
Not to mean cats or dogs.

Xu Niang (speak) No, you must repeat
He who lies must
Be a shameless fellow.

Xu Changmao (speak) Well, well, well,
He who lies must
Be a shameless fellow.

徐　娘　(白)兄长，
请你把前日收回的
扩建南墙的官批牒文
还给小妹。

徐昌茂　(白)牒文！

徐　娘　(白)我要依照官批牒文重葺南墙。

徐昌茂　(白)重葺！

徐　娘　(白)南墙外移——

徐昌茂　(白)移墙！

徐夫人　(白)好哇！

徐昌茂　(白)好什么好！

徐夫人　(白)吔，你要讲话算话哦，
当心变成小狗。

徐　娘　(白)兄长。

徐昌茂　(白)哎哟，妹妹呀，
来来来，

徐昌茂　(唱)姑娘小妹你听我讲，
葺墙为兄来帮忙。
工匠我找最好的派，
材料白送也无妨。

Xu Niang (speak) Dear brother,

Return me the warrant for the

South wall you took back the day before

Yesterday please.

Xu Changmao (speak) Warrant!

Xu Niang (speak) I'll repair the wall according to the warrant.

Xu Changmao (speak) Repair!

Xu Niang (speak) Move it outward—

Xu Changmao (speak) Move it!

Mrs. Xu (speak) Hurrah!

Xu Changmao (speak) Hurrah for what!

Mrs. Xu (speak) Hey, remember you bet that's so,

Otherwise you're shameless.

Xu Niang (speak) Dear brother.

Xu Changmao (speak) Oh, my dear sister,

Come here.

Xu Changmao (sing) Little sister, listen to me,

I'll help you repair the wall.

I'll send you the best workers and

The materials are also free.

万事不用你操心，

保你三天见南墙。

只有一事需依我，

原址、原地，原址原地葺南墙。

徐　娘　（唱）我不要你的钱，

不要你的粮，

里里外外妹妹我都能忙。

只要把公文还给我，

我给你叩头又烧香。

徐昌茂　（唱）你莫瞎讲。

徐　娘　（唱）你要帮忙。

徐昌茂　（唱）我帮不上。

徐　娘　（唱）你也要帮。

徐昌茂　（唱）总得有理扯得上。

徐　娘　（唱）言而无信太荒唐。

徐昌茂　（唱）如今事情有变化。

徐　娘　（唱）公文不还给我，

我，我我……

就跪在你身旁。

徐昌茂　（白）哎哟！

You have nothing to worry about,
You'll see the wall in three days.
But on my condition that
The south wall should be built on the previous site.

Xu Niang (sing) I don't want your money
As well as your rice.
I'm able to cope with anything around my house.
Just return me the document,
I'll burn incense and kowtow.

Xu Changmao (sing) Don't talk nonsense.

Xu Niang (sing) You should help me.

Xu Changmao (sing) I can't help you.

Xu Niang (sing) You have to help.

Xu Changmao (sing) You have to be reasonable.

Xu Niang (sing) It's absurd to eat your words.

Xu Changmao (sing) But at present things have changed.

Xu Niang (sing) If you don't return it,
I'll, I'll, I'll …
Just kneel down beside you.

Xu Changmao (speak) Oh, dear!

徐夫人　（白）哎哟！

徐昌茂　（白）小妹，你起来哟！

徐夫人　（白）小妹，你起来哟！（徐昌茂拉小妹起来，徐夫人按小妹下去）

徐　娘　（白）哥哥喂，

徐　娘　（唱）我从来都听哥哥的话喂，
退还了牒文把哥哥帮。
本为助哥哥把宏呀宏图展，
我青砖白泥就放一旁，放一旁。
到如今风雨突然南墙倒，
书馆里跑光了读书郎。
和成的老病又重犯，
妹妹我如何度日熬时光。
今日你不答应我，
我只能大堂之上去，去……
去悬梁！

徐夫人　（白）哎哟，小妹，
小妹，你不能呢！

徐　娘　（白）嫂子，
你不要拉着我，
让我自己去死。

Mrs. Xu (speak) Oh, dear!

Xu Changmao (speak) Dear sister, stand up please!

Mrs. Xu (speak) Dear sister, stand up please! (Xu Changmao pulls Xu Niang up while Mrs. Xu presses her down)

Xu Niang (speak) My dear brother.

Xu Niang (sing) I have long been obedient with what you said,

So I returned the warrant to help you.

In order to help you realize your ambition,

I agreed to just put aside the blue bricks and white clay.

Now the sudden storm blew down the south wall,

So students ran away from the home school.

And Hecheng has been ill once more,

How can your sister get through the hard days?

Without your promise today,

Then I could only go to the Hall to…

Hang myself!

Mrs. Xu (speak) Oh, my! Sister,

Sister, you can't do that!

Xu Niang (speak) Sister-in-law,

Don't pull me back any more,

Just let me kill myself.

徐夫人　(白)小妹，小妹吔，

有什么大不了的事情，

还要吊颈悬梁哪!

你哥哥他不好办的事情哪，

嫂嫂给你办嘛。

徐昌茂　(白)哎!

你就不要来瞎搅和了。

徐夫人　(白)你能许给张家，

么事不能给小妹家?

徐昌茂　(白)张家?

张家是相府!

徐夫人　(白)那相府也要讲理呀，

墙倒了还不许重修哇?

小妹她不是只要尺把地吗?

徐　娘　(白)不给一尺，

五寸[24]也行。

移过五寸就是金木之地[25]，

再葺南墙

就是一劳永逸了。

徐夫人　(白)看看看，

Mrs. Xu (speak) Dear little sister,

I don't think it is such a big deal

That you are to hang yourself!

Although the thing is difficult for your brother,

I can do it for you.

Xu Changmao (speak) Hey!

You had better not mess up the thing.

Mrs. Xu (speak) You can promise the Zhangs.

Why not promise little sister?

Xu Changmao (speak) The Zhangs?

That's the Minister's!

Mrs. Xu (speak) We should reason things out with them.

How can they not permit rebuilding?

Doesn't she want just a small lot about one chi wide?

Xu Niang (speak) Without one chi,

Five cun[24] is enough.

Five cun outward is the metal and wood land[25].

The rebuilding

Will just be once and for all.

Mrs. Xu (speak) Look, look, look,

只要五寸呢。

徐昌茂　（白）一寸也不行！

徐夫人　（白）我说行！

徐昌茂　（白）这种事又不是菜市场买菜，

还能讨价还价！

徐昌茂　（唱）你们老是长不大，

不懂事理把我缠。

不是我心痛几寸地，

不是我不把妹子帮。

相府扩建事情大，

怎能让她过界葺南墙。

要是她过界，

可能我下班。

这样的事情不能干，

你看不见我的苦衷心里藏。

唉！

徐夫人　（白）哦，弄不好要丢纱帽？

徐昌茂　（白）当然！

徐夫人　（白）下班？

徐昌茂　（白）当然！

She just wants five cun.

Xu Changmao (speak) Not much of anything!

Mrs. Xu (speak) I say yes!

Xu Changmao (speak) Such a thing is not like buying vegetables in the market,

You can't make a bargain!

Xu Changmao (sing) You're always immature and

Unreasonable to haunt me.

Not because I value the lot,

Not because I don't help sister.

The Minister's extension

Is more important than her south wall.

If she crossed the line,

I would be laid off.

I can't do such kind of things for

You don't see the difficulties in my heart.

Alas!

Mrs. Xu (speak) Oh, maybe you will lose your post?

Xu Changmao (speak) Of course!

Mrs. Xu (speak) Laid off?

Xu Changmao (speak) Of course!

徐夫人　（白）那这事办不得噢？

徐昌茂　（白）当然！

徐　娘　（白）兄长，你——

徐夫人　（白）哎哟，小妹吔。

老爷，老爷，

小妹，小妹吔。

徐夫人　（唱）你为你大哥想一想，

别让他头上纱帽黄了汤。

有官无官两个样，

穿鞋总比赤脚强。

公文之事先放下，

多送些银两作补偿。

徐昌茂　（白）你看你看，

你嫂嫂都明白。

这事哥哥不能干，

快去，多拿些银两来。

徐　娘　（白）我真是不该来找你们。

徐夫人　（白）哎，小妹吔，

嫂嫂我给你取银两。

你等着，等着，等着啊。

Mrs. Xu (speak) Then you can not do the thing?

Xu Changmao (speak) Of course!

Xu Niang (speak) Brother, you···

Mrs. Xu (speak) Oh, little sister.

Master, master.

My little sister.

Mrs. Xu (sing) You had better think for your brother,

Don't cause him to lose his official post.

In office or not differs,

In shoes is better than not.

Lay aside the document first,

Let's make you up with more silver.

Xu Changmao (speak) You see, you see,

Your sister-in-law sees it.

Your brother can not do the thing.

Be quick, fetch more silvers for her.

Xu Niang (speak) I really shouldn't come to you for help.

Mrs. Xu (speak) Hey, dear sister,

I'll go to fetch silvers for you.

You just wait for me, wait for me.

等着啊，等着啊！

徐昌茂　（白）小妹呀，

过来过来过来。

唉，

自从和成得病以来，

你在外面争强好胜，

这并不算错。

啊，

可是你趟水过河，

总要问问个深浅吧？

啊？哎！

哥哥许给张家一尺之地，

还不是为了我们徐家

日后有个好前程。

我收回你的官批牒文，

就是怕你惹是生非。

唉，人家是相府，

我们鸡蛋哪能往石头上碰呢？

那小鬼哪里能把阎王捉哇？

徐夫人　（白）小妹，葺墙事大，

Wait for me, wait for me!

Xu Changmao (speak) Dear sister,

Come here, come here, come here.

Well,

Ever since Hecheng became ill, you've

Sought to excel over others outside.

This can not be wrong.

Ah,

But when wade across a river,

Don't you ask it's deep or shallow?

Ah? Hey!

I promised the Zhangs a one-chi-wide lot,

For the purpose that the Xus

Have a prosperous future.

I took back your official warrant,

For fear that you will make trouble.

Well, they're the Minister's

How can we act like striking our eggs against their rocks?

How can little devils dare to catch King of Hell?

Mrs. Xu (speak) Sister, it's a big deal.

嫂子和兄长

也只能出这么个力了。

拿着回家，

记住啊，

是重修不是扩建啊。

拿着，拿着，

哎哟，小妹，

拿着，你拿着呀。

老爷，你看你看，

你不说上几句呀，

小妹她还真不领这个情呢！

徐昌茂　（白）哎呀，小妹呀，

小妹呀，

拿着，拿着吧！

这也是哥哥和嫂嫂的

一点心意嘛。

徐　娘　（白）谢谢兄长嫂子！

徐夫人　（白）俗话说

“鸭肫难剥，人心难摸”，

我看你嘴上心痛小妹，

Your sister-in-law

And brother can only help you with the sum.

Take it back home.

Remember,

It's rebuilding not extending.

Take it, take it.

Alas, sister,

Take it, you just take it.

Master, you see, you see,

If you don't say a few words,

She really will not appreciate your kindness!

Xu Changmao (speak) Alas! Dear sister,

Dear sister,

Take it, just take it!

It's also your brother and sister-in-law's

A little goodwill.

Xu Niang (speak) I'm so grateful to you!

Mrs. Xu (speak) It is said,

"It is hard to detect human mind."

You say you feel pity for sister,

其实全是假的！

徐昌茂 （白）咦！你你你什么意思？

东一下西一下的。

徐夫人 （白）这一回我替你做了回主，

把小妹家的准许扩建南墙的

官批牒文还给小妹着了。

徐昌茂 （白）什么！

徐夫人 （白）我把官批牒文还给小妹着了！

徐昌茂 （白）啊！

徐夫人 （白）哎，老爷，老爷！

来人哪，来人哪！

老爷，老爷！

徐昌茂 （白）你你你，你可坏了我的大事了！

哎哟，快快快，

快去把姑娘给我追回来！

衙役甲 （白）是！

徐夫人 （白）慢，不许追！

徐昌茂 （白）快去，追！

徐夫人 （白）不许追，不许追！

徐昌茂 （白）追！

	It's all false actually!
Xu Changmao	(speak) Hey! What, what, what, what do you mean?
	Just east and west, here and there.
Mrs. Xu	(speak) This time I made a decision for you,
	So just now I returned the official warrant
	For the wall extension to your sister.
Xu Changmao	(speak) What!
Mrs. Xu	(speak) I returned the official warrant to sister!
Xu Changmao	(speak) Ah!
Mrs. Xu	(speak) Hey! Master, master!
	Come here! Come here!
	Master, master!
Xu Changmao	(speak) You, you, you, you just have spoiled my important event!
	Alas, hurry up!
	Chase my sister back for me in a hurry!
Yamen runner A	(speak) Yes!
Mrs. Xu	(speak) Slow down, don't chase!
Xu Changmao	(speak) Be quick, chase!
Mrs. Xu	(speak) Do not chase! Do not chase!
Xu Changmao	(speak) Chase!

徐夫人　（白）不许追，不许追！

徐昌茂　（白）你你你，你这个糊涂鳖！

徐夫人　（白）老爷，老爷！

你可是允许小妹家

扩建南墙在先哪？

现在南墙倒着，

还回公文重修南墙，

也是理所当然。

徐昌茂　（白）哎哟，那老管家……

徐夫人　（白）哎哟，老管家与你是忘年之交，

这点面子还不给你？

再说，

他老管家名为重修相府，

实为扩建占地。

这要是传出去呀，

对相爷的官声也不好啊。

常言说，

“宰相肚里能撑船”，

这么几寸地的事情，

他还能拿你怎么着哇？

Mrs. Xu (speak) Do not chase! Do not chase!

Xu Changmao (speak) You, you, you, you muddled wooden head!

Mrs. Xu (speak) Master, master!

Didn't you allow your little sister

To extend the south wall first?

Now the south wall fell down,

It is also a matter of course

To return the warrant.

Xu Changmao (speak) Alas, the old butler…

Mrs. Xu (speak) Oops, your friendship is between generations,

Can't he give you a little face?

Anyhow,

Namely he rebuilds the Minister's mansion,

In fact he extends it.

If this is to be spread out,

It is not good for the minister's fame.

As they say,

"A Minister is broad-minded."

As to such a small piece of land,

What else can he do to deal with you?

徐夫人　（唱）你把那一捆柴草肩上背，
负荆去把大罪赔。
吴府墙塌妹流泪，
哥哥不能往呀往外推。
许她墙移五寸地，
相府更得好口碑。
老管家会讲“对对对”，
大事小事都会一风吹，
那个吹呀，那个吹呀，
一呀一风吹，一风吹！

徐昌茂　（白）你又要我去负荆请罪[26]？

徐夫人　（白）对！
哎，这不是你最拿手的
老把戏吗？
想当初你想娶，我想嫁，
得罪了我爹爹，
你急得头发根都开了叉。
三天两头负荆来，
叩头作揖说好话。
挨过爹的打，

Mrs. Xu	(sing) You can shoulder that bundle of firewood
	To compensate for your crime.
	She cried for the fallen wall,
	As brother you can't push your sister out.
	If she's allowed to do so,
	The Minister's gets good praise.
	The old butler will say "yes, yes",
	And all the great or small events won't count,
	Won't count at all, won't count at all,
	Will not count at all, not at all!
Xu Changmao	(speak) Want me to offer humble apology[26] again?
Mrs. Xu	(speak) Yes!
	Hey, isn't it the old trick you used to
	Be most skillful?
	At that time we both wanted marriage
	But offended my father.
	You were extremely anxious so you often
	Came with a rod on your back,
	Pleading my father again and again.
	You were hit as well

挨过爹的骂，

我那伤心泪哟，

也流了几大把。

你说受得住忍得下，

这男子汉皮厚，

就是福气大！

徐昌茂 （白）你就给我闭嘴吧！

徐夫人 （白）嗯？

衙役甲 （白）我什么也没有听到！

As blamed by my father.
I also had shed several
Handfuls of heartbroken tears.
You said that you could endure it
Because only the cheeky man
Could have big blessings!

Xu Changmao (speak) For my sake shut up your mouth!

Mrs. Xu (speak) Uh?

Yamen runner A (speak) I did not hear anything at all!

第三场

旁　白　开工喽——

葺一堵南墙高万丈，

葺一堵南墙千里长。

葺一堵南墙避风雨，

葺一堵南墙读文章。

高万丈，千里长，

避风雨，读文章，

来年中个状元郎，状元郎！

徐　娘　（白）伢子们，

南墙葺好，

我们马上开学！

徐　娘　（唱）今日里南墙把工开，

吉祥的紫气东边来。

炮仗冲天响云外，

吉庆的锣鼓，

那个乐呀，那个乐呀，

那个乐呀，那个乐呀，

得儿哟呀子哟，得儿哟呀子哟，

得儿呀子呀子一子哟，

Act III

Voice-over Here we go —
Let's build a south wall to its height,
Let's build a south wall to its length.
Let's build a south wall for shelter,
Let's build a south wall for the school.
To its height, to its length,
For shelter, for the school,
Let's have a Zhuangyuan in the coming year!

Xu Niang (speak) Dear children,
When the wall's done,
We will start school at once!

Xu Niang (sing) Today start building the south wall.
Auspicious air comes from the east.
Crackers roared out of the clouds,
The happy drums and gongs
Are so joyful, are so joyful,
Are so joyful, are so joyful,
De er yo ya zi yo, de er yo ya zi yo,
De er ya zi ya zi yi zi yo,

乐哇乐开怀呀！

徐　娘　（白）茗奴，

快把烧好的茶水

给工匠们送去。

茗　奴　（白）是。

徐　娘　（唱）谁说我吴府钟鼎[27]已不在？

谁说我吴府头难抬？

今日里招牌一块朝外摆，

葺南墙重振家风，

从头再来，从头再来，从头再来！

吴和成　（白）夫人，

葺墙我们就

老老实实葺墙。

放的什么炮仗？

乒乒乓乓锣鼓不嫌吵人？

徐　娘　（白）和成，

别人放得，我们就放得；

别人敲得，我吴府就敲得。

我要的就是这个阵势！

吴和成　（白）么敲得放得，

That we burst into laughter!

Xu Niang (speak) Ming Nu,

Just bring the boiled water and tea

To the craftsmen in haste.

Ming Nu (speak) Yes.

Xu Niang (sing) Who said the Wus had lost our wealth and glory[27]?

Who said the Wus are hard to rise?

Today's rebuilding is a sign for the Wus

To revive the family style

From all over again, from all over again, from all over again!

Wu Hecheng (speak) My dear,

We just build the wall

With no ceremony at all.

Why do you light the crackers?

Don't you think the drums and gongs are too noisy?

Xu Niang (speak) Hecheng.

As long as others light, we can light too;

As long as others knock, the Wus can knock too.

It is just the situation that I want!

Wu Hecheng (speak) Not about knock and light,

你这是与人家较劲。

徐　娘　(白)和成，

自改朝换代以来，

在这桐城县内，

较这股劲的

恐怕不只是我们一家。

吴和成　(白)人家，

人家毕竟是相府。

唉，

时过境迁，

物是人非呀。

你看你看，你看你看，

敲敲打打一个上午，

我也看不出有什么阵势。

连个鬼影子，

也没看到一个。

徐　娘　(白)和成，和成。

众仆役　(白)恭喜恭喜，恭喜恭喜！

恭喜恭喜，恭喜恭喜！

张天昊　(白)哎呀，夫人，

	You're having rivalry with others.
Xu Niang	(speak) Hecheng,
	Since the change of the dynasties,
	In the county of Tongcheng,
	I'm afraid our family
	Isn't the only one to have rivalry.
Wu Hecheng	(speak) Other people,
	After all, are the Minister's.
	Well,
	The passing time
	Makes people different.
	You just have a look, have a look,
	With knocking and beating all morning,
	I can't see any situation you have made either.
	And even I didn't see
	A shadow of ghost at all.
Xu Niang	(speak) Hecheng, Hecheng.
Menservants	(speak) Congratulations! Congratulations!
	Congratulations! Congratulations!
Zhang Tianhao	(speak) Oh, my! Lady Wu,

恭喜恭喜呀!

徐　娘　(白)老管家!

吴和成　(白)哼!

张天昊　(白)来呀,薄礼送上。

仆役甲　(白)是。

徐　娘　(白)慢,

此是何意呀?

张天昊　(白)呃,千金买邻[28]哪。

照相爷惯例,

大喜庆,小喜事,

乡里乡亲要同喜同贺。

今日府上重葺南墙,

老朽略备薄礼,

夫人笑纳。

徐　娘　(白)老管家,你忘了吧,

照惯例我们张吴两府,

可从不在同喜同贺之列呀。

恐怕你送礼是假,

想必是有话要说吧。

张天昊　(白)呵呵呵,聪慧,

Many congratulations!

Xu Niang (speak) Old butler!

Wu Hecheng (speak) Humph!

Zhang Tianhao (speak) Come on, bring the slight gift.

Manservant A (speak) Yes!

Xu Niang (speak) Wait,

For what is your gift?

Zhang Tianhao (speak) Er, for good neighborhood[28].

The Minister is

Used to celebrating the

Happy events with the neighborhood together.

Today you start to rebuild the wall,

So I bring a slight gift.

Take it kindly.

Xu Niang (speak) Old butler, you forget that

Usually the Zhangs and the Wus had never

Celebrated happy events with the neighbourhood together.

I'm afraid you send the gift for

The purpose of saying something.

Zhang Tianhao (speak) Heh, heh, heh, clever enough,

夫人真是聪慧呀。

唉,皇恩浩荡,

相爷荣升……

徐　娘　(白)知道。

张天昊　(白)相爷荣升大学士,

相府老宅还要重修。

徐　娘　(白)明为重修,

实为扩建吧?

张天昊　(白)算是吧。

扩建相府,

乃老夫做主,

徐知县也……

徐　娘　(白)知道!

张天昊　(白)夫人,夫人,

只是有些事情,

还要请夫人行个方便喽。

徐　娘　(白)老管家,

你建你的相府,

与我吴府何干?

再讲,

Lady Wu is really clever enough.
Well, the mighty royal grace,
His promotion…

Xu Niang (speak) I know.

Zhang Tianhao (speak) Because of his promotion,
The old house has to be rebuilt.

Xu Niang (speak) Namely rebuild,
Actually extend?

Zhang Tianhao (speak) Just sort of.
The extension
Is my decision.
And Magistrate Xu…

Xu Niang (speak) I know!

Zhang Tianhao (speak) Lady, lady,
I just want to ask you
To make the things easy for the extension.

Xu Niang (speak) Old butler,
Isn't the Minister's mansion
None of the Wu's business?
What's more,

一个平民百姓，
能给你什么方便哪？

张天昊　（白）扩建相府，
必然涉及这脚下地基。

徐　娘　（白）听管家你的意思是，
我吴府这坍塌的南墙
不能重葺？

张天昊　（白）老朽不是这个意思！
今日一早听得家院来报，
说是吴府画线葺墙
过了地界。
老朽不知是真是假，
前去一看……

徐　娘　（白）出了地界？

张天昊　（白）出了五寸。

徐　娘　（白）不知是出了哪一家的地界？

张天昊　（白）当然是我们……
皇上的，
朝廷的！

徐　娘　（白）老管家，

	As a common person,
	What's that I can make easy for you?
Zhang Tianhao	(speak) The extension
	Must involve the ground work under our feet.
Xu Niang	(speak) So what you are talking about is that
	The collapsed south wall of the Wu's can
	Not be rebuilt?
Zhang Tianhao	(speak) What I talk about does not mean so!
	In the early morning I was reported that
	Your line marking for rebuilding
	Crossed the boundary.
	I don't know if it's true or not,
	And I find it···
Xu Niang	(speak) Crossed the boundary?
Zhang Tianhao	(speak) About five cun out.
Xu Niang	(speak) I don't know whose land boundary the wall crossed out?
Zhang Tianhao	(speak) Of course it is our···
	The emperor's,
	And the court's!
Xu Niang	(speak) Old butler,

我吴府移墙，

只因南墙屡屡坍塌。

根结所在，

就是地基软烂。

外移五寸，

只是为了南墙不倒。

张天昊 （白）你进了五寸，

就坏了我的大事了！

徐　娘 （白）坏了你的大事？

张天昊 （白）重修相府。

徐　娘 （白）扩建。

张天昊 （白）扩建相府

乃老朽心愿，

衙门所定。

老朽垂暮之年

也就为相爷

做此一件大事了。

徐　娘 （白）那我？

张天昊 （白）你倒墙重葺，

只能在原址之上。

I move the wall just

Because the south wall often collapsed.

It is due to

The rotten foundation.

Move it five cun out

So that the south wall won't fall again.

Zhang Tianhao (speak) You moved it five cun in,

But it spoiled my important event!

Xu Niang (speak) Spoiled your important event?

Zhang Tianhao (speak) The rebuilding.

Xu Niang (speak) Extending.

Zhang Tianhao (speak) The extension

Is my only desire

Set by Yamen.

In my declining years,

It's the only thing I

Can do for the Minister.

Xu Niang (speak) Then I?

Zhang Tianhao (speak) You have to rebuild

The wall on the formal site.

现在你进了五寸，
相府如何开工？
夫人，你改址葺墙，
只能退，不能进！

徐　娘　（白）只能退，不能进？

徐　娘　（唱）皇上的土，
朝廷的地，
谁敢犯一寸一厘？
衙门里面摆事理，
早准我五寸之外为墙基。
你历来做事都仔细，
这一回文章可是走了题！

张天昊　（唱）夫人说话别生气，
有理无须来扯皮。
你明明占了五寸地，
怎说我话儿走了题？
若是衙门许给你，
当有个牒文契约和官批。

徐　娘　（白）当然有。

张天昊　（白）拿来老朽一看。

Now you moved it five cun in,
How can I start the work?
Lady Wu, you can change the site,
Not forward but backward!

Xu Niang (speak) Not forward but backward?

Xu Niang (sing) Emperor's earth,
The land of court,
Who dares offend a little?
Bring out reasons in Yamen,
I was allowed to extend the wall base.
You always do things carefully,
But this time what you wrote is off the topic!

Zhang Tianhao (sing) Don't be angry with my words for
We don't need to argue about it.
Clearly it's you who took the land,
Why do you say I missed the topic?
If Yamen granted it to you,
You should have the official documents.

Xu Niang (speak) Of course I have.

Zhang Tianhao (speak) Take here to have a look.

徐　娘　(白)非得给你一看?

张天昊　(白)听夫人的口气,
你墙出五寸
是经过衙门准许的了?

徐　娘　(白)你讲呢?

张天昊　(白)说句不怕夫人多心的话,
老朽未见衙门牒文,
不能相信!

徐　娘　(白)说句老管家不高兴的话,
老管家要看衙门牒文,
衙门里查去。

张天昊　(白)你,
讲得好,讲得好!
夫人,
就算你有衙门牒文,
老朽也能将它变成
一纸空文!

众仆役　(白)对!

徐　娘　(白)莫非老管家仗持相府,
不把我们平民百姓

Xu Niang (speak) You have to have a look?

Zhang Tianhao (speak) Listen to what you say,
You move it five cun out
With the approval of the Yamen?

Xu Niang (speak) In your view?

Zhang Tianhao (speak) What I say does not mean to make you touchy.
If I don't see Yamen warrant,
I can't believe it!

Xu Niang (speak) What I say means to make you unpleasant.
If you want to see Yamen warrant,
Check it in Yamen.

Zhang Tianhao (speak) You,
Well said! Well said!
Lady Wu,
Even though you have Yamen warrant,
The dotage can also turn it into
A dead letter!

Menservants (speak) Right!

Xu Niang (speak) Is it possible that you depend on
The Minister and think nothing

放在眼里?

张天昊 (白)哎哟!

徐　娘 (白)南墙开工,

我就不陪你老人家了。

你送来的贺礼呀,

我也就不客气了。

张天昊 (白)夫人,夫人,夫人!

你硬是要葺,

也是沙上建塔,

故意寻灾觅祸哇!

气死我了,气死我了!

徐知县!徐昌茂——

徐昌茂 (白)来着——

张天昊 (白)你!

徐昌茂 (白)老管家,

你看下官不是背着柴草

负荆请罪来着吗?

张天昊 (白)请你个头哇!

你负荆为的是来作秀,

你,你你你请罪要的是滑头!

Of common people?

Zhang Tianhao (speak) Goodness!

Xu Niang (speak) The south wall starts,
So I will not be with you any more.
As to the gift you give me,
I will accept it bluntly.

Zhang Tianhao (speak) Lady, lady, lady!
If you insist on it,
You're building tower on sands
And causing disaster on purpose!
Make me so mad! Make me so mad!
Magistrate! Xu Changmao—

Xu Changmao (speak) Coming—

Zhang Tianhao (speak) You!

Xu Changmao (speak) Old butler,
Don't you see I'm shouldering the firewood
To ask for your punishment?

Zhang Tianhao (speak) Punish your head off!
You shoulder firewood to make a show,
And you, you ask for punishment to play tricks!

立马改过还是好朋友，
一意孤行结怨仇。
这顶戴，
这花翎，
多抢手！
别有福不求，
把祸求！

徐昌茂　（白）老管家！

张天昊　（白）你是趁相府扩建，
浑水摸鱼以权谋私，
还是想故意
败坏相爷的声名？

徐昌茂　（白）老管家，
我们再作商议，再作商议。

张天昊　（白）哪个与你商议，
你让她马上停工！

众仆役　（白）停工！

徐昌茂　（白）停工！

张天昊　（白）拆墙！

众仆役　（白）拆墙！

Mend your ways at once, we're still good friends.

Go your own way, we have grudge.

How much in

Demand the

Trappings are!

Don't pray for trouble but

No blessing!

Xu Changmao (speak) Old butler!

Zhang Tianhao (speak) Do you take advantage of

The extension for private gains,

Or ruin on purpose

The fame of the Minister?

Xu Changmao (speak) Old butler,

Let us discuss it again, discuss it again.

Zhang Tianhao (speak) Who will discuss it with you?

Tell her to stop work right now!

Menservants (speak) Stop work!

Xu Changmao (speak) Stop work!

Zhang Tianhao (speak) Tear down!

Menservants (speak) Tear down!

徐昌茂　(白)拆墙!

张天昊　(白)两天以后,
若是不见动静,
老朽将八百里快马[29]
修书进京。
将你言而无信
做下的荒唐之事,
报与相爷。
到时,
不知你有几个脑袋
供朝廷砍杀?

徐昌茂　(白)老管家,老管家!
老管家,
你可千万不能这么做哇。
报与相爷就是报与皇上,
报与皇上,
那卑职的身家性命……

张天昊　(白)既然知道这些利害,
就该少做一些这样的
荒唐之事!

Xu Changmao (speak) Tear down!

Zhang Tianhao (speak) Two days later,
Suppose nothing happens,
I'll send to the capital a letter
Of urgency[29].
Report the absurd thing
Of your eating of your words
To the Minister.
By then,
I don't know how many heads you have
For the court to chop?

Xu Changmao (speak) Old butler, old butler!
Old butler,
You can never report it whatever happens.
Your report means the emperor would know,
Then all the life
Of my family and I would be…

Zhang Tianhao (speak) Now that you know the gains and losses,
You are supposed to do fewer of such
Ridiculous things!

徐昌茂　(白)糊涂,卑职糊涂!

　　我这就派人去吴府!

张天昊　(白)我怕你是躲不过亲情!

徐昌茂　(白)我,我我我能大义灭亲!

张天昊　(白)大义灭亲?

徐昌茂　(白)大义灭亲!大义灭亲。

张天昊　(白)一言为定!

徐昌茂　(白)一言为定!

张天昊　(白)呵呵呵呵!

Xu Changmao (speak) Confused, I am confused!

I'm sending someone to the Wu's house.

Zhang Tianhao (speak) I'm afraid you can't avoid your family love!

Xu Changmao (speak) I, I, I, I can place justice above!

Zhang Tianhao (speak) Place justice above?

Xu Changmao (speak) Place justice above! Place justice above!

Zhang Tianhao (speak) That is a deal!

Xu Changmao (speak) That is a deal!

Zhang Tianhao (speak) Ho ho ho ho!

第四场

徐昌茂　(白)老班头!

衙役甲　(白)哎——来着!

徐昌茂　(白)快,快!

衙役甲　(白)老爷,么事呀?

徐昌茂　(白)快去请你家姑娘过府议事!

衙役甲　(白)啊?

徐昌茂　(白)快去请你家姑娘过府议事!

衙役甲　(白)哦,是是是!

徐昌茂　(白)快快快!

小班头,小班头!

衙役乙　(白)来着!

徐昌茂　(白)快快,快去看看你家姑娘

怎么还没有来呀?

衙役乙　(白)是!

徐昌茂　(白)快!(衙役乙跑)

你快一点喏,你快一点喏!

衙役甲　(白)老爷——

老爷,姑娘请不动。

徐昌茂　(白)请不动?

衙役甲　(白)奉命去请。

Act IV

Xu Changmao	(speak) Old head runner!
Yamen Runner A	(speak) I'm coming!
Xu Changmao	(speak) Hurry! Hurry!
Yamen Runner A	(speak) What's the matter, master?
Xu Changmao	(speak) Hurry to ask my sister here for discussion!
Yamen Runner A	(speak) Pardon?
Xu Changmao	(speak) Hurry to ask my sister here for discussion!
Yamen Runner A	(speak) Oh, yes yes yes!
Xu Changmao	(speak) Get moving!
	Young head runner, young head runner!
Yamen Runner B	(speak) Coming!
Xu Changmao	(speak) Hurry up and have a look at my sister.
	Why has she not come here yet?
Yamen Runner B	(speak) Yes!
Xu Changmao	(speak) Hurry! (Yamen Runner B runs away)
	You'd be in a hurry! You'd be in a hurry!
Yamen Runner A	(speak) Master—
	Master, your sister doesn't come.
Xu Changmao	(speak) She doesn't come?
Yamen Runner A	(speak) I invited her.

姑娘讲，

动手葺墙她要监工。

徐昌茂　（白）啊？

衙役乙　（白）老爷，老爷！

徐昌茂　（白）人呢？

衙役乙　（白）姑娘家里里外外

忙个不停，

南墙已经动手开工了。

徐昌茂　（白）开工了？

衙役乙　（白）开工了！

徐昌茂　（白）这么快？

难道你没讲

南墙的事还没有敲定？

衙役乙　（白）讲过了。

徐昌茂　（白）那兄长请她来

是要从长计议？

衙役甲、乙　（白）也讲着。

徐昌茂　（白）她不肯前来？

衙役乙　（白）不肯前来。

（徐昌茂疾走，心生一计，以扇击掌）

	But she said
	She had to oversee the building.
Xu Changmao	(speak) What?
Yamen Runner B	(speak) Master, master!
Xu Changmao	(speak) Where's she?
Yamen Runner B	(speak) She has been busy all the time
	Inside and out
	For they have started building the south wall.
Xu Changmao	(speak) Have they started?
Yamen Runner B	(speak) Yes, they have!
Xu Changmao	(speak) They're so fast?
	Didn't you tell her that
	The issue of south wall was undecided yet?
Yamen Runner B	(speak) Yes, I did.
Xu Changmao	(speak) And I invited her for
	A further discussion?
Yamen Runner A and B	(speak) Yes, we did.
Xu Changmao	(speak) Would she not come yet?
Yamen Runner B	(speak) No, she would not.
	(Xu Changmao walks around quickly; suddenly he has an idea, tapping his hand with his folding fan.)

徐昌茂　　(白)那,你们就讲老爷我死着。

衙役甲、乙　　(白)老爷死着?

徐昌茂　　(白)我是她的兄长,
活的不见,
死的还不见哪?

衙役甲　　(白)老爷的主意
就是老爷的主意!
真叫绝!
不过,
你这么一个大大的活人,
怎就好好的死掉着?
你这不是阎王爷贴布告——
鬼话连篇嘛。

徐昌茂　　(白)你是讲姑娘不信?

衙役乙　　(白)是的嘛,我都不信,哪个信喏?

徐昌茂　　(白)衙门给你发薪水,
就让你长膘不长心哪?
你难道不能帮老爷我扯几句?
你们就讲老爷为着南墙
气的、急的、

Xu Changmao	(speak) Well, you just tell her your master is dead.
Yamen Runner A and B	(speak) Is the master dead?
Xu Changmao	(speak) Since I am her elder brother, Not seeing me alive, Will she not see me dead?
Yamen Runner A	(speak) The idea of master Is really the master's idea! Wonderful! But Actually you are such a live wire; How can you die in a sudden? Isn't it like the King of Hell posting a notice, Telling a pack of lies?
Xu Changmao	(speak) You mean she won't believe it?
Yamen Runner B	(speak) Yes, of course. Even I don't believe it; how about others?
Xu Changmao	(speak) You are paid by Yamen not To use your brain but fatten you up? Can't you help your master by telling a few false words? You just say for the south wall, I was so Angry and anxious,

恼的、焦的、
喝闷酒醉死的！

衙役甲、乙　（白）讲你喝闷酒
醉死了？
老爷，
你可是一斤[30]不倒，
两斤不摇，
酒里能做梦，
酒里能睡觉，
从来也没有醉过啊！

徐昌茂　（白）笨猪！
你们就讲，
老爷我喝的是假酒嘛！

衙役甲、乙　（白）好！这个主意好！
好！

徐昌茂　（白）快给老爷把事办了！
快去！去！

衙役甲、乙　（白）是！是！

徐昌茂　（白）一个大活人，
不夸自己升官发财，

	Annoyed and afraid
	That I had drunk myself to death!
Yamen Runner A and B	(speak) Tell her that you had
	Drunk yourself to death?
	Master,
	You're not tipsy with one jin[30] spirits,
	Not malty with two.
	You can dream in spirits
	And even sleep in spirits.
	So you have never got drunk at all!
Xu Changmao	(speak) Stupid!
	You just say that
	Your master drank the adulterated spirits!
Yamen Runner A and B	(speak) Great! This is a great idea!
	Great!
Xu Changmao	(speak) Hurry to tackle this for your master!
	Go quickly!
Yamen Runner A and B	(speak) Yes! Yes!
Xu Changmao	(speak) A live wire doesn't praise
	His promotion and fortune but

却非得咒自己死。

好？好什么好？

徐夫人　　(上)老爷！

红中白板清一色，

杠上开花一条龙！[31]

我赢着！赢着！赢着！

徐昌茂　　(白)你赢着，我输了！

徐夫人　　(白)你又不会打牌，

你输么东西？

徐昌茂　　(白)我输前程！

徐夫人　　(白)输前程？

徐昌茂　　(白)你可闯了大祸了！

衙役甲、乙　　(白)姑娘到！

徐昌茂　　(白)小妹来着。

徐夫人　　(白)小妹来着。

徐昌茂　　(白)屋里头讲。

徐夫人　　(白)小妹来着。

徐昌茂　　(白)屋里头讲。

徐夫人　　(白)她来找你。

徐昌茂　　(白)她来哭我的。

	Has to curse himself to death.
	Great? What the hell is great?
Mrs. Xu	(onstage) Master!
	Red dragon, white dragon, pure one suit,
	And a complete sequence from 1 to 9![31]
	I won it! I won! I won!
Xu Changmao	(speak) You won, but I lost!
Mrs. Xu	(speak) You do not play mahjong.
	What's the thing you lost?
Xu Changmao	(speak) I lost prospects!
Mrs. Xu	(speak) Lost prospects?
Xu Changmao	(speak) You really got me into trouble!
Yamen Runner A and B	(speak) Here comes your sister!
Xu Changmao	(speak) Little sister is coming.
Mrs. Xu	(speak) Little sister is coming.
Xu Changmao	(speak) Come in and talk.
Mrs. Xu	(speak) Little sister is coming.
Xu Changmao	(speak) Come in and talk.
Mrs. Xu	(speak) She comes to see you.
Xu Changmao	(speak) She comes to mourn me.

徐夫人　　(白)她来哭你?

徐昌茂　　(白)我死着嘛!

徐夫人　　(白)你死着?

你讲么胡话哦?

衙役甲、乙　(白)姑娘到!

徐昌茂　　(白)屋里头讲,屋里头讲。

徐　娘　　(唱)忽听衙役报丧信,

徐娘难禁热泪淋。

嘴里虽有万千恨,

难躲心里血脉情。

徐夫人　　(哭)老爷,老爷!

徐　娘　　(唱)争争吵吵亲情在,

一死万念俱成空。

徐夫人　　(哭)小妹!

徐　娘　　(哭)嫂子!

徐夫人　　(哭)小妹!

徐　娘　　(哭)嫂子!

哥哥,嫂子!

徐昌茂　　(白)小妹!

人死不能复生,

Mrs. Xu	(speak) Come to mourn you?
Xu Changmao	(speak) For I've been dead!
Mrs. Xu	(speak) You've been dead?
	What wild talk are you talking?
Yamen Runner A and B	(speak) Here comes your sister!
Xu Changmao	(speak) Come in and talk. Come in and talk.
Xu Niang	(sing) Hearing the sudden death news,
	Xu Niang can't help shedding tears.
	Though I spoke how I hate him,
	I can't resist family love.
Mrs. Xu	(cry) Master! Master!
Xu Niang	(sing) Family love exists in quarrels,
	But everything is crushed by death.
Mrs. Xu	(cry) Little sister!
Xu Niang	(cry) Sister-in-law!
Mrs. Xu	(cry) Little sister!
Xu Niang	(cry) Sister-in-law!
	Brother! Sister-in-law!
Xu Changmao	(speak) Little sister!
	As the dead can't revive,

你我都要节哀自重，

莫要哭坏了身子哟！

徐　娘　（哭）嫂子，哥哥！

嫂子！

徐　娘　（唱）兄长的好处讲不尽，

徐昌茂　（唱）讣告里面出好人。

徐　娘　（唱）忘不了里里外外暗帮衬，

徐昌茂　（唱）手足情骨肉情情意深深。

徐　娘　（唱）想当年大红花轿桐城进，

徐昌茂　（唱）我驮着妹妹上轿下轿泪淋淋。

徐　娘　（唱）抬腿步子放不下，

徐昌茂　（唱）一脚踩碎一颗心。

徐　娘　（唱）恨我太任性，

徐昌茂　（唱）恨我太无能。

徐　娘　（唱）恨风雨倒南墙，

徐昌茂　（唱）恨兄长驴技穷。

徐　娘　（唱）悔不该逼得紧，

徐昌茂　（唱）也怪我没说清。

徐　娘　（唱）今日一道南墙夺兄命，

徐昌茂　（唱）假戏真做难成真。

You and I should restrain our grief.

Don't fall ill due to oversorrow.

Xu Niang (cry) Sister-in-law! Brother!

Sister-in-law!

Xu Niang (sing) My brother's merits are too many to tell.

Xu Changmao (sing) People were perfect in their obits.

Xu Niang (sing) I can't forget his secret help for me.

Xu Changmao (sing) We are tied by blood kinship so closely.

Xu Niang (sing) I entered Tongcheng in my wedding sedan-chair.

Xu Changmao (sing) I carried her on and off the sedan-chair with tears.

Xu Niang (sing) He was loath to part with me.

Xu Changmao (sing) Each step was like breaking a heart.

Xu Niang (sing) I hate being willful.

Xu Changmao (sing) I hate being helpless.

Xu Niang (sing) I hate the fall-down wall.

Xu Changmao (sing) I hate having no other tricks.

Xu Niang (sing) I regret forcing him hard.

Xu Changmao (sing) And I should be blamed too.

Xu Niang (sing) Today a south wall took away my brother's life.

Xu Changmao (sing) It's hard to make a false play.

徐　娘　(唱)早知南墙一移留悔恨，

我争什么五寸与三分？

徐　娘　(哭)嫂子！

徐夫人　(哭)小妹！

徐夫人　(白)哎哟，小姑奶奶喂！

你呀就是太倔太犟。

要是早让你哥哥一步，

何至于有今天？

徐　娘　(白)嫂子！

非是小妹倔犟，

小妹如此作为实出无奈，

心中另有隐情啊。

徐夫人　(白)这话怎讲啊？

徐　娘　(白)我家和成，

不背祖训情系大明。

竹杖芒鞋云游在外，

十载有零。

如今身缠重病药石无能，

偌大吴府如油灯尽，

大厦倾。

Xu Niang (sing) Had I known the regretful result,

I would not have stuck to move the wall.

Xu Niang (cry) Sister-in-law!

Mrs. Xu (cry) Little sister!

Mrs. Xu (speak) Oops, my little grandaunt!

You are just too tough and stubborn.

If you had yielded to your brother earlier,

Would it have been like this?

Xu Niang (speak) Sister-in-law!

I'm not tough nor stubborn.

I had no choice but to insist on it

Due to a hidden secret.

Mrs. Xu (speak) What makes you say so?

Xu Niang (speak) My man, Hecheng,

Has followed his family teachings

And wandered around far from home for

More than ten years.

Now he suffers from incurable disease.

So big the Wu's is on the wane

And declines.

三年来，
为和成寻医问药，
不辞苦辛日以继夜，
如影随形。
晓之以理动之以情，
他终念我夫妻情意，
渐渐走出迷津。
与我开馆授徒，
著书立说以终其身。
今日若是让了南墙，
和成以为是屈从清廷。
小妹能让，
和成难以相容。
三年苦苦劝慰，
将是过眼烟云。
和成正在康复，
更有发病可能。
若再离家出走，
哪里还有吴府？
小妹又将何从？

For three years
I have sought treatment for him,
Sparing no trouble all day and night.
Being his shadow and
Talking about reasons and affection,
I've reminded him of our love and
Helped him get away from astray.
Now he teaches students and
Is an author for his remaining years.
If I had given way to them today,
He'd have thought it a yield to the Court.
I can do it,
But it's hard for Hecheng.
Then three years' efforts and
Comforts would be in vain.
Hecheng is getting well,
But attacks are likely.
Were he away from home again,
Where would the Wu's still exist?
Where should your sister go?

再建南墙，

不能让只能进，

这是吴家脸面所在，

也是为了

我那青梅竹马的夫君！

徐　娘　(唱)和成他病得太久太久，

只留下西风孤楼。

往事不堪回首，

只盼春上枝头。

徐夫人　(白)小妹，小妹！

徐　娘　(唱)一切从头开始，

找回诗酒唱酬。

埋葬亡国之恨，

过那笔墨春秋。

耕读是人根本，

寒窗能解忧愁。

谁知事起南墙，

把人生悔恨万世留。

徐夫人　(白)小妹，小妹！

徐昌茂　(白)小妹！

The south wall can

Only be rebuilt outwards.

This is the face of the Wus and

It is also for

My dear husband and childhood sweetheart!

Xu Niang (sing) Hecheng has been ill for too long, leaving

A building alone in west wind.

It's hard to look back and

I hope for a good future.

Mrs. Xu (speak) Little sister!

Xu Niang (sing) Let's start a new life with

Writing and drinking again.

Let's bury the hatred and

Have a scholarly life.

Study and farming is basic;

Hard learning is carefree.

Who knows that the south wall

Brings about eternal regret to life.

Mrs. Xu (speak) Sister, sister!

Xu Changmao (speak) Sister!

徐　娘　　　　（白）哥哥！

徐夫人、徐昌茂　（白）小妹！

徐　娘　　　　（白）嫂子！

徐昌茂　　　　（白）小妹，你听我讲。

徐夫人　　　　（白）小妹，小妹！

徐　娘　　　　（白）你不是死着吗？

徐夫人　　　　（白）他是死着，

你来着这么一哭，

又把他哭活着。

徐昌茂　　　　（白）对对对！

徐　娘　　　　（白）原来你报的是假丧！

徐　娘　　　　（唱）伤心泪白白来流淌，

气得我真是咬断了牙！

乌鸦难得报佳音，

衙门从来无真话！

手足情你也逗着耍，

哪里配头戴纱帽，

人五人六坐县衙？！

徐昌茂　　　　（白）小妹，你听我讲。

徐　娘　　　　（白）告诉你，衙门大印我盖着，

Xu Niang	(speak) Brother!
Mrs. Xu and Xu Changmao	(speak) Sister!
Xu Niang	(speak) Sister-in-law!
Xu Changmao	(speak) Sister! Listen to me.
Mrs. Xu	(speak) Sister, sister!
Xu Niang	(speak) But you were dead, weren't you?
Mrs. Xu	(speak) Yes, he was dead. But you came here and mourned him, He was brought back to life!
Xu Changmao	(speak) Yeah, yeah! Yeah!
Xu Niang	(speak) So you reported a false funeral!
Xu Niang	(sing) My sad tears were shed for nothing. So annoyed that I bit my teeth off! Crows are rare to bring good news; And truth never exists in Yamen! You even teased my emotion for you. How can you deserve the post And put on airs in Yamen?
Xu Changmao	(speak) Sister! Listen to me.
Xu Niang	(speak) Just tell you that since I have the warrant

文牒官批我拿着，

南墙我不但要葺，

我还要厚二尺高三丈！

徐昌茂　（白）小妹！

徐夫人　（白）小妹，小妹！

徐昌茂　（白）奴才！

衙役甲　（白）老爷！

徐昌茂　（白）准备柴草。

衙役甲　（白）又去相府？

徐昌茂　（白）对，再去相府过招！

这一回，

我得要拿下顶子，

脱下袍子，

为我那苦命的妹子。

张天昊　（白）徐知县，徐昌茂！

徐昌茂　（白）来着！

With Yamen's official seal,

I'll not only build the south wall,

But also make it thicker and taller!

Xu Changmao (speak) Sister!

Mrs. Xu (speak) Sister, sister!

Xu Changmao (speak) Minion!

Yamen Runner A (speak) Master!

Xu Changmao (speak) Prepare firewood!

Yamen Runner A (speak) Go to the Minister's again?

Xu Changmao (speak) Right! Go there to dispute again.

This time I'd

Take off my official cap

And gown to help

My very bitter little sister.

Zhang Tianhao (speak) Magistrate Xu, Xu Changmao!

Xu Changmao (speak) Coming!

第五场

张天昊　（白）徐知县扯了个
大义灭亲的谎，
把一个缓兵之计将我诳！
相爷修书问情况，
老朽心里发了慌。
徐知县，徐昌茂！

徐昌茂　（白）来着！

张天昊　（白）来了？

徐昌茂　（白）来着！

张天昊　（白）又驮了几根柴草？

徐昌茂　（白）又驮了几根柴草。

张天昊　（白）负荆请罪？

徐昌茂　（白）负荆请罪。

张天昊　（白）两天期限已到，
你玩的什么花招？

徐昌茂　（白）两天期限已到
本县不敢玩花招，
只是有话要同老管家讲。

张天昊　（白）讲！

Act V

Zhang Tianhao	(speak) Magistrate Xu lied that
	He would place justice above,
	Cheating me with a trick to gain more time.
	The Minister wrote for progress,
	Getting me into a panic.
	Magistrate Xu, Xu Changmao!
Xu Changmao	(speak) Coming!
Zhang Tianhao	(speak) Coming?
Xu Changmao	(speak) Coming!
Zhang Tianhao	(speak) Just with a few firewood again?
Xu Changmao	(speak) Just with a few firewood again.
Zhang Tianhao	(speak) Make amends with rods?
Xu Changmao	(speak) Make amends with rods.
Zhang Tianhao	(speak) The two-day limit was due.
	What tricks on earth are you playing?
Xu Changmao	(speak) The two-day limit was due.
	I dare not to play any tricks.
	I just want to speak a few words with you.
Zhang Tianhao	(speak) Speak!

徐昌茂　（唱）老管家，

你一腔怒火且按下，

听一听小县令唠唠家常。

做买卖想的是万千家产，

做官的想的是千古名扬。

相爷他，

一步一步官儿越做越大。

相爷他，

对百姓对邻里世上无双。

他做官在人上，

他做人在人下。

有了这个下，

才有那个上。

一上一下讲究大，

你我都要把相爷做榜样！

遇事多为他人想，

为百姓吃点亏受点屈，

比什么都强。

张天昊　（白）绕来绕去想说什么？

徐昌茂　（白）你没听明白？

Xu Changmao (sing) Old butler,

Dam up your anger for the moment.

Give an ear to the magistrate's chit-chat.

Businessmen want to own a large fortune,

While officials want a long-lasting fame.

The Minister

Has been higher officials step by step.

The Minister

Has been the best to the people and neighbors.

His post is above others but

His modesty is below others.

If without this "below",

There is no that "above".

"Above" and "below" need careful study.

You and I are supposed to learn from him!

Think for others whatever happens.

Suffering losses and wrongs for people is

Better than anything.

Zhang Tianhao (speak) What do you mean in a roundabout way?

Xu Changmao (speak) Don't you catch the point?

张天昊　(白)什么意思!

徐昌茂　(白)张吴两府相邻的那几寸地皮,

本县做主,请相府容让。

张天昊　(白)容让?给哪个?

徐昌茂　(白)西后街的徐娘。

张天昊　(白)呸!

小老鼠拖蛮槌——

大头在后。

徐知县!

徐昌茂　(白)老管家!

张天昊　(白)徐昌茂!

徐昌茂　(白)张总管!

张天昊　(白)老朽这里再大,(以手指胸)

也容不得你如此地戏弄!

徐昌茂　(白)老管家若是怕有牵累,

有苦我受,有罪我扛!

还请相府容让五寸。

张天昊　(白)你胆子不小哇!

我要你敦促拆墙,

你要我让地,

Zhang Tianhao	(speak) What do you mean?
Xu Changmao	(speak) About the lot adjacent to the Zhang's and the Wu's, I decide to ask you to concede.
Zhang Tianhao	(speak) Concede? To which one?
Xu Changmao	(speak) Xu Niang in west Backstreet.
Zhang Tianhao	(speak) Pah! A mouse drags a wooden club— The rear is big. Magistrate Xu!
Xu Changmao	(speak) Old butler!
Zhang Tianhao	(speak) Xu Changmao!
Xu Changmao	(speak) Steward Zhang!
Zhang Tianhao	(speak) Even I have a broad mind, (point at his bosom) I cannot put up with your tricks like that!
Xu Changmao	(speak) If you were afraid of the coming trouble, I'd bear the suffering and blame! Please concede five-cun land to them.
Zhang Tianhao	(speak) You have got such a nerve! I ask you to urge the tearing, But you ask me to give way.

你分明是以权谋私！

徐昌茂　（白）利为百姓谋，

举贤不避亲。

小妹也是百姓黎民，

我身为朝廷的衙门，

我不能失信于民。

望老管家，

体察本县苦衷，

代为向相爷禀明！

张天昊　（白）如此说来，

这墙是不让的了？

徐昌茂　（白）无相让之情！

张天昊　（白）不拆了？

徐昌茂　（白）无再拆之理！

张天昊　（白）你你你想好了？

徐昌茂　（白）我想好了！

卑职这里修书一封，

烦请老管家捎带进京，

前因后果全写在这信上了！

张天昊　（白）哈哈哈！

	You're abusing your power for personal gains!
Xu Changmao	(speak) I seek gains for people
	Not avoiding relatives.
	My sister is also one of them.
	As an official of the court,
	I can't lose the trust of people.
	I hope you can
	Consider my difficulties
	And report it to the Minister!
Zhang Tianhao	(speak) Therefore you mean
	She will not concede the wall?
Xu Changmao	(speak) No reason for conceding!
Zhang Tianhao	(speak) No tearing down?
Xu Changmao	(speak) No reason for tearing!
Zhang Tianhao	(speak) You··· have you thought it over?
Xu Changmao	(speak) Yes, I have!
	I've already written a letter
	Which could be brought to the capital please.
	The entire process is all in the letter!
Zhang Tianhao	(speak) Ha ha ha!

你也修书？

也配修书？

还修书进京！（相府众仆役笑，张天昊撕信）

徐昌茂　（白）哎，你怎么撕了它？

你你你！

张天昊　（白）呸！（掷信）

张天昊　（唱）我说你难把亲情躲，

你说你能唱大义灭亲歌。

到头来谎言自戳破，

害了自己涮了我。

真想把你剁三剁，

靠着南墙把酒喝。

徐知县！徐昌茂！

该修怎样的书信，

老朽自然明白。

来呀！

众仆役　（白）在！

张天昊　（白）八百里快马即刻进京！

众仆役　（白）是！

张天昊　（白）你，你就等着好消息吧！

	You've written a letter?
	Are you qualified?
	"Bring it to the capital"! (Menservants burst into laughter; Zhang Tianhao tears up the letter.)
Xu Changmao	(speak) Hay, how can you tear it up?
	You, you, you!
Zhang Tianhao	(speak) Pah! (He throws pieces around)
Zhang Tianhao	(sing) I said you can't avoid family love,
	But you told me you can place justice above.
	In the end, your lies poked themselves,
	Biting yourself and fooling me.
	I do want to chop you up,
	Have a drink against the south wall.
	Magistrate Xu! Xu Changmao!
	About how to write the letter,
	Of course the old man knows.
	Come here!
Menservants	(speak) Here!
Zhang Tianhao	(speak) Ride the fastest horse to the capital at once!
Menservants	(speak) Yes!
Zhang Tianhao	(speak) You, you're just waiting for the good news!

徐昌茂　(白)老管家,老管家!(仆役簇拥老管家下)

徐昌茂　(唱)坏着了喂!

老管家烈火浇油,烧着了喂!

坏着了喂!

徐昌茂运交华盖,把祸招喂!

本想是把

相府小心服侍好,

为亲情为小妹支上一招。

岂知是麦秸草箍鸭蛋,

一头也够不着!

懊恼!懊糟!懊恼!懊糟!

懊糟!懊恼!懊糟!懊恼!

旁白　(唱)呀子一子喂!

一子呀子哟!

懊恼!懊糟!

徐昌茂　(白)唉!

我多想

夫妻好,

邻里好,

官情好,

Xu Changmao (speak) Old butler, old butler! (Old butler leaves with menservants.)

Xu Changmao (sing) It's really bad!

Old butler is as angry as burning with oil!

It's really bad!

Xu Changmao has bad luck to court disaster!

I planned to serve

The Minister's well with care

And give an idea to sister for kinship.

Who knew it's like tying duck eggs with straws—

No one end can be met!

Furious! Upset! Furious! Upset!

Upset! Furious! Upset! Furious!

Voice-over (sing) Ya zi yi zi wei!

Yi zi ya zi yo!

Furious! Upset!

Xu Changmao (speak) Gosh!

How I wish

Loving couples,

Good neighbors,

Nice officials,

亲情好，

你好，我好。

徐昌茂　（唱）大家都好！

徐昌茂　（白）恨只恨这堵墙，

太大！太高！

太厚！太重！

徐昌茂　（唱）憋得我手上无招，

南墙、北墙、

白泥、灰砖，

你你你你们来凑什么热闹！

徐昌茂　（白）我真想拳打脚踢，

把这南墙、北墙、高墙、矮墙、

厚墙、薄墙、大墙、小墙、

南墙、北墙、

高墙、矮墙、

厚墙、薄墙、

大墙、小墙、

看得见的摸不着的、

看不见的推不倒的、

鬼打墙[32]，

Fine kinship.

You're fine, I'm fine.

Xu Changmao (sing) Everyone is fine!

Xu Changmao (speak) I just hate this wall is

Too huge! Too high!

Too thick! Too heavy!

Xu Changmao (sing) I'm too pent-up to have ideas.

South wall, north wall,

White clay, gray bricks,

Why are you all here to add trouble to me alone?

Xu Changmao (speak) I do want to punch and kick

These south wall, north wall, high wall and low wall,

Thick wall, thin wall, huge wall, small wall,

South wall, north wall,

High wall, low wall,

Thick wall, thin wall,

Huge wall, small wall,

Even the visible and untouchable,

Or invisible, indestructible

Ghost-hit-wall[32],

一把推倒！

徐昌茂　(唱)做一个美梦逍遥！

旁白　(唱)呀子一子喂，

一子呀子哟，

美梦逍遥！

徐昌茂　(白)只可惜，

徐昌茂　(唱)葫芦按不下，

眼前全是瓢。

旁白　人之初，性本善。

性相近，习相远。

苟不教，性乃迁。

教之道，贵以专。

昔孟母，择邻处。

徐　娘　(唱)月煌煌，夜风凉，

墙边蛩吟，

塘里蛙唱。

一声一应，

一声一应。

真叫我，

无限惆怅，涌进心房。

All shove them down!

Xu Changmao (sing) Then I will have a good dream!

Voice-over (sing) Ya zi yi zi wei,

Yi zi ya zi yo,

Have a good dream!

Xu Changmao (speak) It's a pity

Xu Changmao (sing) That I failed to solve

Troubles one after another.

Voice-over Man on earth, good at birth.

The same nature, varies on nurture.

With no education, there'd be aberration.

To teach well, you deeply dwell.

Then Mencius' mother, chose her neighbor.

Xu Niang (sing) With shining moon and chilly breeze,

Crickets are chirping,

Frogs are singing.

Their singing and

Responding make

Me really

Filled with infinite melancholy.

几天来与相府一场较量，
赢来了一尺一尺长南墙。
虽说是工地上无风无浪，
我心里是风急浪又狂。
赢得南墙又怎样？
输了南墙又何妨？
来来去去赌口气，
细细想来多荒唐。
想当年，
我夫妻也算得齐眉举案，
南墙边诗词酬唱，
常到天亮。
鸿鹄之志在心上，
只盼春风好扬帆。
岂知道世事多变化，
沧海桑田[33]梦醒黄粱[34]。
无奈何撑起了吴家天地，
风雨中学会了好胜争强。
心里总是空荡荡，
梦里也觉人凄凉。

During these days, my contest against the Zhangs
For the building land wins a long south wall.
Although it seems peaceful and uneventful,
I am extremely anxious and stressed.
What about winning the south wall?
Does it matter if I lose?
Being at odds repeatedly is
Too ridiculous after thinking!
In those years,
We could be loving and respectful couple,
Often writing poems together by
South wall until dawn.
He cherished lofty ambition,
Only hoping for a good chance.
Who knew dramatic changes happened[33]
And woke us up from wishful dreams[34]?
I had no choice but to prop up the Wus,
Learning to win and compete in struggles.
In my mind it's always empty;
In my dreams I'm also desolate.

看着这一湾清水，
对着明月银光，
手抚双鬓流热泪，
倍加失落与彷徨。
我多想时光如水能倒淌，
重做回，
无忧无虑、
无牵无挂未嫁的小姑娘。

吴和成　（白）夫人！

徐　娘　（白）和成，你怎么来了？

吴和成　（白）夫人！
我怕你害怕，
就跟了过来。

徐　娘　（白）和成！和成！（相拥）

吴和成　（白）夫人！夫人！
是我拖累了你呀！
夫人，我们不争了。
我们换个地方，
换一个没有什么
南墙北墙的地方。

Looking at this bay of clear water,
Facing silvery moonlight
Touching temples tearfully,
I feel doubly lost and restless.
How I wish time could flow upstream like water.
Then I could
Be a carefree
Fancy-free unmarried little girl again

Wu Hecheng (speak) Darling!

Xu Niang (speak) Hecheng, why do you come here?

Wu Hecheng (speak) Darling!
I'm afraid you are scared,
So I follow you.

Xu Niang (speak) Hecheng, Hecheng! (They hug each other)

Wu Hecheng (speak) Darling, darling!
It's me who's a drag on you!
Darling, let's quit struggling
And move to another place,
A place where there is no such
Things like south walls or north walls.

徐　娘　(白)这世界上还有

没有墙的地方吗?

吴和成　(白)有,

我想会有。

只是我们没有去找。

只要我们执意去找,

就能找到

没有南墙北墙的地方。

唉,我是个没有用的男人。

我说的话你也许不信。

徐　娘　(白)信!

和成,我信!

Xu Niang	(speak) Is there still in the world
	Such a place without any walls?
Wu Hecheng	(speak) Yes.
	I believe it.
	We just don't start to look for it.
	As long as we insist on looking,
	We'll be able to
	Find a place without south or north walls.
	Well, since I am a useless man to you,
	Maybe you don't believe what I said
Xu Niang	(speak) No!
	I believe you!

第六场

众仆役　(白)哎——相爷修书回家啰!
　　　　相爷修书回家啰!
张天昊　(唱)这书信多气派!
众仆役　(唱)多呀多气派!
张天昊　(唱)我真是舍不得来打开,
众仆役　(唱)舍不得开也要开。
张天昊　(唱)我真想压在那个枕头下面,
众仆役　(唱)压在枕头下面,
张天昊　(唱)梦里也能,哈哈哈哈哈哈,笑开怀!
众仆役　(唱)笑喂笑喂,笑呀么笑开怀!
张天昊　(唱)这书信多精彩!
众仆役　(唱)多呀多精彩!
张天昊　(唱)能引百万大军来!
众仆役　(唱)大军来呀大军来!
张天昊　(唱)更有摧枯(那个)拉朽势哎!
众仆役　(唱)摧枯拉朽势!
张天昊　(唱)天下都归我安排!
众仆役　(唱)你呀你呀,你呀么你安排,你安排!
张天昊　(白)快看,看!

Act VI

Menservants (speak) Aha—the Minister has written back! The Minister has written back!

Zhang Tianhao (sing) What a stylish letter!

Menservants (sing) How stylish it is!

Zhang Tianhao (sing) I really do not want to open it.

Menservants (sing) Anyway you have to open it.

Zhang Tianhao (sing) I really want to put it under my pillow.

Menservants (sing) Put it under your pillow.

Zhang Tianhao (sing) I would laugh out, ha ha ha ha ha ha, in my dreams!

Menservants (sing) Laugh out, laugh out, laugh out loud heartily!

Zhang Tianhao (sing) What a powerful letter!

Menservants (sing) How powerful it is!

Zhang Tianhao (sing) It can draw millions of troops!

Menservants (sing) Millions of troops will come here!

Zhang Tianhao (sing) Its power can overcome everything so easily!

Menservants (sing) Overcome so easily!

Zhang Tianhao (sing) The world's arranged all by me!

Menservants (sing) It's you, it's you, it's you who is to arrange the world!

Zhang Tianhao (speak) Look at this!

相爷的家书！

相爷的家书！

老朽哪想修书进京？

哪想修书进京？

只是吴府

太不把我放在眼里！

乡绅甲　(白)哎,老管家！

你已经做到仁至义尽了嘛！

张天昊　(白)嗯！

乡绅乙　(白)像这样的人家,

早就应该这样地对付他了！

众　人　(白)嗯！

乡绅丙　(白)他这是咎由自取,

不得好报！

众　人　(白)嗯！

张天昊　(白)咎由自取？

众　人　(白) 咎由自取！

张天昊　(白)不得好报？

众　人　(白) 不得好报！

张天昊　(白)哈哈哈哈哈！

The Minister's letter!

The Minister's letter!

I didn't want to write to the capital!

Not want to write to him!

But the Wus have

Never taken me seriously too much!

Squire A (speak) Ah, old butler!

You have already shown them extreme tolerance!

Zhang Tianhao (speak) Yeah!

Squire B (speak) As to such a family,

You should have dealt with them earlier in this way!

All the roles (speak) Yeah!

Squire C (speak) They really deserve the blame,

No good reward!

All the roles (speak) Yeah!

Zhang Tianhao (speak) Deserve the blame?

All the roles (speak) Deserve the blame!

Zhang Tianhao (speak) No good reward?

All the roles (speak) No good reward!

Zhang Tianhao (speak) Ha ha ha ha ha!

仆役甲　(白)老管家,快把书信打开!

仆役乙　(白)有相爷撑腰,
还怕他不拆南墙?

仆役丙　(白)要灭他吴家九族!

仆役甲　(白)嗯!要他滚出我桐城县!

众乡绅　(白)老管家,快把书信打开吧!
看看!

张天昊　(白)打开?(问右侧众人)

众　人　(白)打开!

张天昊　(白)打开?(问左侧众人)

众　人　(白)打开!

张天昊　(白)打开!(开匣阅信,晕倒)

众　人　(白)哎,老管家,老管家!(众乡绅阅信)

乡绅甲　(白)好!妙!哈哈哈哈哈!

旁　白　千里修书只为墙,
让他三尺又何妨?
长城万里今犹在,
不见当年秦始皇!

徐　娘　(唱)忽闻相府把墙让,
徐娘心里乱如麻。

Manservant A	(speak) Old butler, open the letter quickly!
Manservant B	(speak) The Minister backs us. Are we still afraid they refuse?
Manservant C	(speak) Kill all of their relatives!
Manservant A	(speak) Yeah! Get them out of our Tongcheng County!
Squires	(speak) Old butler, open the letter quickly and Read it!
Zhang Tianhao	(speak) Open it? (He asks people on the right)
All the roles	(speak) Open it!
Zhang Tianhao	(speak) Open it? (He asks people on the left)
All the roles	(speak) Open it!
Zhang Tianhao	(speak) Open it! (He opens the box and reads the letter, then faints)
All the roles	(speak) Ah, old butler, old butler! (Squires read the letter.)
Squire A	(speak) Good! Fine! Ha ha ha ha ha!
Voice-over	Write to me just for a wall. Why not offer him three chi land? Now the Great Wall still stands there, But the First Emperor doesn't exist!
Xu Niang	(sing) Hearing the news of conceding, I'm at a loss what to do.

吴和成　(唱)说什么惊天动地事情大，
忽觉得脸上火辣辣。

徐　娘　(唱)道什么权不怕来势不怕，
总觉得让人笑掉牙。

吴和成　(唱)是他赢了我？

徐　娘　(唱)还是我赢了他？

吴和成　(唱)谁能讲得清？

徐　娘　(唱)谁能来解答？

吴和成　(唱)往日里三步两步到墙下，

徐　娘　(唱)今日里腿重千斤，
抬不起它。

吴和成　(唱)千里修书只为墙，
让他三尺又何妨？
长城万里今犹在，
不见当年秦始皇！

吴和成　(白)千里修书只为墙，
让他三尺又何妨？
让，让，让，让！
哈哈哈！哈哈哈！

徐　娘　(白)和成！

Wu Hecheng	(sing) You say it is something earth-shaking; now
	Suddenly my face became hot.
Xu Niang	(sing) I say we are not afraid of the power;
	I always feel we are laughed at.
Wu Hecheng	(sing) Did he win me out?
Xu Niang	(sing) Or did I win him out?
Wu Hecheng	(sing) Who can make it clear?
Xu Niang	(sing) Who can answer it?
Wu Hecheng	(sing) In the past a few steps could reach the wall.
Xu Niang	(sing) Today my legs are so heavy that
	I can't lift them.
Wu Hecheng	(sing) Write to me just for a wall.
	Why not offer him three chi land?
	Now the Great Wall still stands there;
	But the First Emperor doesn't exist!
Wu Hecheng	(speak) Write to me just for a wall.
	Why not offer him three chi land?
	Offer, offer, offer, offer!
	Ha ha ha! Ha ha ha!
Xu Niang	(speak) Hecheng!

吴和成　(白)夫人,我想明白了!

我想明白了!

吴和成　(唱)他让你也让,

他强你更强!

人争一口气,

佛争一炉香。

争来争去争个理,

理在谦让中藏。

争一回斗一场,

争争斗斗是笑谈!

徐　娘　(白)和成,你说什么?

吴和成　(唱)九九归一一本账,

万物和谐日月长。

徐昌茂　(白)讲得好,讲得好!

徐　娘　(白)兄长,嫂子!

徐昌茂　(白)姑爷!

吴和成　(白)舅爷!

徐昌茂　(白)姑爷!

吴和成　(白)舅爷!(上前行礼)

徐昌茂　(白)姑爷,你……哈哈哈哈!(同行礼,两人笑倒)

Wu Hecheng (speak) Darling, I have thought it through!

I have thought it through!

Wu Hecheng (sing) You do as he does.

You're better than he!

Man lives for one breath

Buddhas for disciples.

We have argued to make sense but

The sense hides in the courtesy.

All arguments and fights

Will become a laughing stock!

Xu Niang (speak) Hecheng, what are you saying?

Wu Hecheng (sing) In the end it is the same.

Harmony makes the world better.

Xu Changmao (speak) Well said! Well said!

Xu Niang (speak) Brother, sister-in-law!

Xu Changmao (speak) Brother-in-law!

Wu Hecheng (speak) Brother-in-law!

Xu Changmao (speak) Brother-in-law!

Wu Hecheng (speak) Brother-in-law! (He steps forward and bows to him.)

Xu Changmao (speak) Brother-in-law, you… Ha ha ha ha! (They both bow and laugh out.)

吴和成　（白）舅爷，姑爷我告诉你一个秘密。

徐昌茂　（白）哦？（两人挪近）

吴和成　（白）舅爷，这世界本无边无际，
可姓王也可姓张。

徐夫人　（白）也可以姓我们家的徐嘛！

徐昌茂　（白）对对对！
谁做皇帝都是一样，
只要把老百姓记在心里呀！

吴和成　（白）所有的墙哪都不该用砖葺！

徐夫人　（白）对，用篱笆，篱笆透气！

徐昌茂　（白）去！
姑爷的意思是说，
这世上就不该有墙。

吴和成　（白）墙高，墙低，墙厚，墙薄，
全在人的心里。

徐夫人　（白）啊吔，全部放在心里，
那不把人给憋死着啊！

徐昌茂　（白）对，聪明人有时是糊涂，
那糊涂人更有高人一着的棋呀！
那相爷的诗……

Wu Hecheng	(speak) Brother-in-law, I have a small secret to tell you.
Xu Changmao	(speak) What? (They move closer.)
Wu Hecheng	(speak) Brother-in-law, the original boundless world Can be the Wangs' or the Zhangs'.
Mrs. Xu	(speak) It can also be the Xus' from our family!
Xu Changmao	(speak) That is right! No matter who is the emperor, As long as he keeps common people in his mind!
Wu Hecheng	(speak) All the walls should not be built of bricks anymore!
Mrs. Xu	(speak) Yes, use a fence which lets air in.
Xu Changmao	(speak) No! What brother-in-law said means that There should not be walls in the world.
Wu Hecheng	(speak) Tall or low, thick or thin, the walls Exist in the hearts of the people.
Mrs. Xu	(speak) Aya, all walls exist in the hearts. How can those people not be pent-up yet?
Xu Changmao	(speak) Yes, clever people sometimes may be foolish; While a fool sometimes may produce a superior idea! The minister's poem···

吴和成　　(白)药!

徐昌茂　　(白)药?(起身思忖,恍然大悟)

好药!好诗!

吴和成　　(白)好诗!好药!

徐夫人　　(白)你看他们!

一下子药一下子诗的

你们两个大男人,

也要做个主呀,

你看这个南墙……

吴和成、徐昌茂　　(白)南墙,哈哈哈哈哈!(相拥而舞)

千里修书只为墙,

让他三尺又何妨?

长城万里今犹在,

不见当年秦始皇!(下)

徐　娘　　(唱)一瞬间换了天和地,

神使鬼差真叫奇!

多少个日落又日起,

多少回月换又星移。

劝不了夫君回心转意,

走不出恩恩怨怨一盘棋。

Wu Hecheng (speak) Cure!

Xu Changmao (speak) Cure? (He stands up and ponders, then sees light suddenly.)

Good cure! Good poem!

Wu Hecheng (speak) Good poem! Good cure!

Mrs. Xu (speak) Just look at them!

At one time cure and at another poem,

Since you two are big men,

You should make a decision.

You think the south wall should…

Wu Hecheng and Xu Changmao (speak) South wall? Ha ha ha ha ha! (They dance together)

Write to me just for a wall.

Why not offer him three chi land?

Now the Great Wall still stands there;

But the First Emperor doesn't exist! (They go offstage.)

Xu Niang (sing) Everything has changed in a sudden.

How strange and amazing it is!

How many days and nights have gone by?

How many seasons and years have passed?

I couldn't persuade him to change his mind.

He was lost in the maze of resentment,

放不下吴府的节与义，
忘不了为南墙争高争低。
到头来家书一封传千里，
前嫌尽释心旷神怡。

徐　娘　（白）伢子们，
我们推倒它！
伢子们，
我们推倒它！

徐　娘　（唱）推倒它！推倒它！
莫让它挡住太阳！
推倒它！推倒它！
莫让它挡住眼光！
让春风吹进新绿，
让春光带来灿烂。
让浮云薄雾散尽，
让我们乘风扬帆。
让我们推倒狭隘，
让我们迎来宽敞。
让我们推倒怨恨，
让我们迎来吉祥。

Not setting aside the Wu's integrity,
Not forgetting to struggle for south wall.
In the end the minister's home letter
Made us feel forgivable and fresh.

Xu Niang (speak) All the kids,
Let's pull down the wall!
All the kids,
Let's pull down the wall!

Xu Niang (sing) Pull it down! Pull it down!
Don't let it blot out the sun!
Pull it down! Pull it down!
Don't let it blot out our view!
Let the breeze paint the yard green;
Let the spring bring here brilliance.
Let the clouds and mist disperse;
Let us set sail in the wind.
Let us overcome narrowness;
Let us welcome spaciousness.
Let us overcome bitterness;
Let us welcome happiness.

让我们推倒邪恶，
让我们迎来善良。
让我们推倒隔阂，
让我们迎来体谅。
推倒！推倒
所有的不和谐，
迎来歌舞升平，
国泰民安，
处处喜洋洋！

旁　白　（唱）千里修书只为墙，
让他三尺又何妨？
长城万里今犹在，
不见当年秦始皇！
千里修书只为墙，
让他三尺又何妨？
长城万里今犹在，
不见当年秦始皇！

旁　白　天能丈，
地能量。
难量丈，

Let us overcome viciousness;
Let us welcome kindheartedness.
Let us overcome estrangement;
Let us welcome forgiveness.
Overcome! Overcome
All of the disharmony;
Welcome the peacefulness
And prosperity;
Everywhere is cheerful!

Voice-over (sing) Write to me just for a wall.
Why not offer him three chi land?
Now the Great Wall still stands there;
But the First Emperor doesn't exist!
Write to me just for a wall.
Why not offer him three chi land?
Now the Great Wall still stands there;
But the First Emperor doesn't exist!

Voice-over Universe can
Be measured;
But it's hard

一个让。

敬一尺，

还一丈。

你也让，

我也让。

天更宽，

地更广。

天能丈，

地能量。

难量丈，

一个让。

—剧　终—

注:本书相应完整演出视频可在以下网址观看 https://v.qq.com/x/page/o05125xqskt.html

For courtesy.
Offer one chi;
Take one zhang.
You and me,
Be courtly.
Universe will
Be broader.
Universe can
Be measured;
But it's hard
For courtesy.

—The End—

Note: The complete performance video can be watched on the following website https://v.qq.com/x/page/o05125xqskt.html

注释 Notes

1.桐城派:Tongcheng School,the largest essay genre in the Qing Dynasty in China, is also known as "Tongcheng Ancient School", usually called as "Tongcheng School".

2.三朝宰相:the Prime Minister for Three Emperors,that is the Prime Minister for the Emperor Kangxi, the Emperor Yongzheng and the Emperor Qianlong of the Qing Dynasty.

3.尺:*Chi* (a traditional Chinese unit of length, equal to 1/3 meter)

4.三字经:This part is the beginning of *Three Character Primer*. Its translation is made by Professor Zhao Yanchun from Tianjin Foreign Studies University.

5.傩戏:The Nuo Opera, known as the "living fossil of Chinese drama", is one of the oldest cultures in China. It is a kind of drama formed by folk songs and dances and dramas based on folk rituals, popular in provinces like Anhui, Jiangxi, Hubei, Hunan, Sichuan, Guizhou, Shaanxi and Hebei, etc.

6.秀才:*Xiucai* (one who passed the lowest imperial examination at the county level in the Ming and Qing dynasties)

7.文华殿大学士:The Grand Secretary of Wenhua Hall was

used to coach the Crown Prince. In the Qing Dynasty, the cabinet system of the "Three Halls and Three Courts" gradually evolved. The Grand Secretary of Wenhua Hall became the assistant of the Emperor to manage the government affairs, and governed the officials. The authority was greatly extended compared with that in the Ming Dynasty.

8.老朽:the dotage, a modest word often used by an old man to call himself in ancient China

9.万岁:His Majesty. Originally the Chinese term meant to exist forever, or was used as the words of congratulations to the monarch. It is also used today as a tribute to express highly appreciative emotional slogans. In Chinese feudal society, the term is synonymous with the supreme ruler.

10.知县:magistrate. It was the name of an ancient local official. In the Song Dynasty, those officials in the capital who were sent to rule counties were called "the official who knows affairs in a county", abbreviated as Zhixian. In the Ming and Qing dynasties it was the official name of county administrative officials.

11.丈:*zhang*, a traditional Chinese unit of length, equal to 10 *chi*.

12.大人:similar to my Lord, a term of respect for the senior

13.黄道吉日:an auspicious day or a zodiac day, a special word in the Chinese traditional calendar, which refers to the days when all things are appropriate.

14.乌鸦嘴:corvine mouth, a person who has a lot of words and is annoying.

15.生姜还是老的辣: similar to the western saying that veterans are wiser than recruits. It is a common saying in Chinese which means old people are experienced and do things skillfully. It can also be likened to the maturity or perfection of things in some aspects.

16.满堂彩:a Chinese figurative metaphor and positive evaluation of the effect of a good performance.

17.姑爷:a form of address for son-in-law by the family of his wife.

18.翰林:*Hanlin*, a member of the Imperial Academy.

19.状元:*Zhuangyuan* or number one scholar, a title conferred on the one who came first in the highest imperial examination.

20.大学士:*Daxueshi*, the grand secretary of the council during the Qing Dynasty.

21.地煞对天罡:*Disha* to *Tiangang*. Chinese Taoism says there are 36 *Tiangang* stars in the Beidou cluster, each of which represents a god, with a total of 36 gods. When the Taoists practiced the magic arts, they were often called down to exorcise ghosts.*Disha* is a general term for evil spirits and a metaphor for evil forces, usually with a total of 72. In the view of Taoists, *Tiangang* is the main blessing, and *Disha* is the main culprit.

22.犯相:The traditional Chinese believe that if the zodiac and life palace of husband and wife violate each other, it is harmful for their marriage and family.

23.花翎:peacock plume, usually worn by the royal families and

the ministers of high ranks in the Qing dynasty as hat decoration.

24.寸:*cun*, a traditional Chinese unit of length, equal to 1/30 metre.

25.金木之地:a metal and wood land. In Chinese Taoism, everything in the world can be divided into five elements (metal, wood, water, fire and earth). A metal and wood land is a prosperous land.

26.负荆请罪:bearing the rod and willingly taking the punishment—to offer a humble apology; or bring a rod on one's back and ask for punishment. This is a famous Chinese idiom. During the Warring States period, Lin Xiangru, an official in Zhao State, was ordered to go out to Qin State, and he did not disgrace his mission. Later, he accompanied the King of Zhao State to meet the King of Qin State at Mianchi and helped the King of Zhao State avoided insult from the King of Qin State. The King of Zhao State highly praised Lin Xiangru and appointed him as the prime minister. The General Lian Po was very dissatisfied with this, so he repeatedly told others that he would humiliate Lin Xiangru while the latter took sick leave and tried not to meet him. Later, when Lian Po learned that the prime minister's actions were entirely based on national affairs, he felt so shameful that he offered a humble apology with a rod on his back to ask for punishment. After they got united, they tried their best to help the King of Zhao State govern the state well.

27.钟鼎之家: the house of wealth and glory. This word originates from the Chinese idiom "钟鸣鼎食". In the ancient China, when the powerful family and honourable nobility had dinner, they would play clocks and put a variety of precious food in lots of cooking vessels with two loop handles and three or four legs. Therefore, this idiom is used to describe the luxury of the power and the luxurious life of the rich family.

28. 千金买邻: spend a lot of money to buy good neighbors. This is an allusion with the metaphor that it is hard to have good neighbors. It is recorded that in the Northern and Southern Dynasties, a well known man named Lv Senzhen was respected and loved by people. Because Lv Senzhen was honest, noble, resourceful and courageous, people were willing to approach and talked with him. A retired official bought a house next door to Lv Senzhen's house at the cost of one thousand one hundred *liang* silver. When Lv Senzhen was astonished at the expensive cost, the man said with a smile: "One hundred *liang* is used to buy a house, and that one thousand *liang* is used to buy a neighbor."

29. 八百里快马: In ancient times, the file transfer was based on stations. Generally, there was a station every 20 li (li, a traditional Chinee unit of length, equal to 500 meters). Once the words to be delivered were marked on the official document, it must be delivered at a speed of 300 li per day. In the event of an emergency, the speed of delivery can reach 400 li per day, 600 li per day, and up to 800 li. When passing emergency documents, each station uses fast horses. The "eight hundred li of expedition" is dedicated to the information transmission in an emergency.

30. 斤: *jin*, a traditional Chinese unit for measuring weight,

equal to 0.5 kilogram.

31.红中白板清一色,杠上开花一条龙:red dragon, white dragon, pure one suit, and a complete sequence from 1 to 9. These are English terms for mahjong from 麻将中英文术语大全 http://www.sohu.com/a/205679990_559507

32.鬼打墙:The so-called "ghost-hit-wall" means that when walking at night or in the suburbs, the direction cannot be distinguished and the self-perception is vague, so one doesn't know where to go and is always in the same place. When telling such experiences to others, it is difficult for others to understand, so it is called "ghost- hit-wall". In fact, this is a state of hazy consciousness of people.

33.沧海桑田:This is a Chinese idiom, meaning that the sea turns into farmland and the farmland becomes the sea. It is a metaphor for people in the world to change greatly, or to change faster, and to describe changes over time.

34.梦醒黄粱:Here 黄粱 refers to yellow rice, and this means when he wakes up from the dream, the yellow rice has not cooked. According to legend, during the Tang dynasty, a priest named Lv Weng met a young scholar named Lu Sheng who was eager to get rich and wealthy. Lv Weng's persuasion didn't work, so he asked Lu Sheng to sleep on a pillow, letting him get rich and glory in his dreams. Lu Sheng experienced big ups and downs in his dreams, and finally spent the rest of his life in the prosperity of wealth. Lu Sheng woke up after finishing his dream and found that the steamed yellow rice of the owner was not cooked. The idiom has been passed down to the present, and it is used to compare the prosperity of a glory to a dream, short and illusory.